THE KING'S PEACE
1637–1641

C. V. WEDGWOOD

THE KING'S PEACE

1637-1641

THE GREAT REBELLION

COLLINS FONTANA

First published by William Collins Sons & Co. Ltd. 1955
First issued in the Fontana Library 1966
Second Impression November 1968
Third Impression November 1970
Fourth Impression April 1971
Fifth Impression May 1972

To

GEORGE MACAULAY TREVELYAN, O.M.

Printed in Great Britain
Collins Clear-Type Press
London and Glasgow

CONTENTS

CONTENTS

ILLUSTRATIONS

ACKNOWLEDGEMENT

Although this book has been in my mind for many years it would not have been finished by 1954—if finished at all—without the perfect conditions for work generously given to me by the Institute for Advanced Study, Princeton. I would like to take this occasion of expressing my admiration for the Institute and its work under the humane guidance of Dr. Robert Oppenheimer and my gratitude to my friends there, more especially to the late Professor Edward Meade Earle—without whose kindly persistence in urging me to cross the Atlantic I should not have enjoyed those months of exhilarating and peaceful endeavour.

INTRODUCTION

The King's Peace is a narrative history of the British Isles for the four years in the reign of King Charles I which immediately preceded the Civil Wars. I hope in later volumes to describe the course of these wars and the Republican experiment that followed them. The story is not simple; it involves three separate countries, England, Scotland and Ireland, and two civilisations of a wholly different type, the Normanised Anglo-Saxon and the Celtic.

The Scots first revolted against the King because he would have compelled them to religious conformity with England. The Irish next rose, not against the King, but against English and Scottish settlers and the aggressive Protestantism of the English Parliament. They established an independent government at Kilkenny for upwards of eight years. The English, who appealed last to arms, fought—with assistance and diversions from the Scots, Irish and Welsh—a war for religious and political principles which ended in the death of the King on a public scaffold. This, being much resented in Scotland, precipitated a war within Scotland and another between Scotland and England.

European governments, aware of the strategic importance of the British Isles in their own wars, intervened with open or secret help. The French, the Dutch and the Danes offered to mediate between King Charles and his subjects. The Pope sent his nuncio, and the Kings of France and Spain sent their ambassadors to the Irish at Kilkenny. A German prince fixed hopeful eyes on the not quite vacant English throne. English settlements in the Netherlands, Scottish settlements in the Baltic, groups of English traders in Leghorn, Constantinople and Madras felt the far vibrations of the war. So did the young colonies on the eastern fringe of America's vast continent, and the island outposts in the West Indies.

The civil wars of the British Isles had an effect on European politics, on the dominion of the Mediterranean and the rise and decline of colonial empires, but essentially they were the intimate concern of our islands and sprang from the explosive energy, diverse ideals and colliding interests of their inhabitants. The principles for which they fought and the problems that they tried to solve are alive to-day; the conflict between the authority of the State and the liberty of the subject, between public responsibility and private conscience is not, and probably never will be, fully resolved. The doctrines they created, the laws they made or unmade, the sufferings and triumphs of individuals, their nobility and their baseness—all are part of the tradition we inherit and within which we live and think. We are still so much involved with this conflict that passion and propaganda colour all that has been written about it. It is not yet an academic study which we can approach with scientific indifference and cannot become so while a vital current of continuous belief runs through it to us. The final, dispassionate, authoritative history of the Civil Wars cannot be written until the problems have ceased to matter; by that time it will not be worth writing.

A writer approaching a controversial and lively subject on which much has been written owes it to the reader to make his own position at least as clear as it is to himself. The causes of the Civil Wars have been analysed, the rights of the combatants have been judged and weighed by Churchman and Dissenter, Whig and Tory, Liberal and Marxist, utilitarian and romantic. The religion, the political morality and the philosophies of his own time colour the outlook of every writer, however conscientious, although, wise in his own generation, each may add something to our understanding of the past. No historian has ever been, or will ever be, omniscient in his knowledge or infallible in his deductions. None can see the whole and undivided truth.

The contemporary could not do so either. Puzzled by the variety of events which came so confusingly upon him from day to day, and ignorant of much that time alone would bring to light, he steered his way through his own world—as we do now—by the imperfect judgment of an ill-informed mind. But the contemporary knew one thing that the historian can only imagine: he knew what it felt like to be alive at that time, to experience those religious doubts, political fears, and economic pressures as a part of his life. He may not have known or suspected influences which have been later revealed; but he knew what he experienced in his mind or suffered in his flesh, and he knew what beliefs and what interests he admitted to be the motives of his action. "Here we are subject to error and misjudging one another," said Strafford on the scaffold. The day-to-day events of history arise at least in part from error and misjudgment. On this level falsehood itself is a part of truth.

Before history can be put into a coherent perspective it is often necessary to clear away the misinterpretations and the half-knowledge by which contemporaries lived. But the application of modern methods of research, together with modern knowledge and prejudice, can make the past merely the subject of our own analytical ingenuity or our own illusions. With scholarly precision we can build up theories as to why and how things happened which are convincing to us, which may even be true, but which those who lived through the epoch would neither recognise nor accept. It is legitimate for the historian to pierce the surface and bring to light motives and influences not known at the time; but it is equally legitimate to accept the motives and explanations which satisfied contemporaries. The two methods produce different results, but each result may be a fair answer to the particular question that has been asked. They become misleading only if either is accepted as the whole truth.

I have not attempted in this book to examine underlying causes, but rather to give full importance and value to the admitted motives and the illusions of the men of the seventeenth century. I have sought to restore their immediacy of experience.

History experienced is not simple for those who experience it, as every intelligent inhabitant of the twentieth century is aware, and it is impossible to express the full significance of contemporary confusion without sacrificing some, though I hope not all, appearance of clarity. I have tried to describe the variety, vitality and imperfections as well as the religion and government of the British Isles in the seventeenth century in an opening section, deliberately avoiding analysis and seeking rather to give an impression of its vigorous and vivid confusion. Otherwise this book is intended as a straightforward and chronological narrative. I have preferred to describe events as far as possible in the order in which they happened, although this necessarily means a shifting of interest from theme to theme and from place to place. A narrative which sorts out the muddled strands of day-to-day events makes smoother reading, but only a resolute insistence on chronology can make the immediate pressures and confusions which acted on contemporaries clear to the modern reader.

The highest ideals put forward in this generation of conflict were noble; the men who fought or worked for them were less noble than the ideals, for the best of men do not consistently live on the highest plane of virtue, and most men live far below it. The idealisation of certain figures in the Civil War has led, later, to exaggerated condemnations, but a cynical view of human frailty is no help to the historian, and human values can be fairly assessed only if an honest effort is made to understand the difficulties and prejudices of each of the people concerned. These mental acrobatics cannot always be successful, but the attempt to perform them is always illuminating.

This book covers only a few years, and many of the people in it cannot be fully understood until their lives are seen as a whole. It is my aim to show the unfolding of certain characters and the emergence of others and to comment on them, as far as possible, from evidence relating only to the years described. Clarendon's account of Charles I, for instance, together with most of the best known descriptions of the King, belong to a later epoch, are coloured by the knowledge of his end, and are therefore misleading if their evidence is allowed to influence a study of him as he was between the years 1637 and 1641.

The behaviour of men as individuals is more interesting to me than their behaviour as groups or classes. History can be written with this bias as well as another; it is neither more, nor less, misleading. The essential is to recognise that it answers only one set of questions in only one way. Few methods of historical study do more, and no harm will be done by any of them so long as the limitation is understood. This book is not a defence of one side or the other, not an economic analysis, not a social study; it is an attempt to understand how these men felt and why, in their own estimation, they acted as they did.

BOOK ONE

THE HAPPIEST KING IN CHRISTENDOM

June 1637

We have no other intention but by our government to honour Him by Whom Kings reign and to procure the good of our people, and for this end to preserve the right and authority wherewith God hath vested us.

Charles I

O thou, that dear and happy isle,
The garden of the world erewhile,
Thou Paradise of Four Seas
Which Heaven planted us to please,
But – to exclude the world – did guard
With wat'ry, if not flaming, sword:
What luckless apple did we taste
To make us mortal and thee waste?

Andrew Marvell

I. COURT AND COUNTRY

Charles, King of Great Britain and Ireland, in the thirty-seventh year of his age and the thirteenth of his reign, believed himself to be the happiest King in Christendom. He said as much in the warm June of the year 1637 to his eldest nephew and godson, the Elector Palatine, Charles Louis, who with his next brother Rupert had been on a long visit to his Court. They were the sons of the King's only sister Elizabeth, whose husband, once Elector Palatine and King of Bohemia, had lost in the German wars all that he possessed.

King Charles's claim was not extravagant. He was, to all immediate observation, singularly blessed in the inward tranquillity and the outward peace of his dominions. He had not wished to be involved in the bloody turmoil of Europe even for his sister's and her children's sake. As one of his many courtier poets had prettily expressed it:

> Tourneys, masques, theatres better become
> Our halcyon days; what though the German drum
> Bellow for freedom and revenge, the noise
> Concerns not us, nor should divert our joys;
> Nor ought the thunder of their carabins
> Drown the sweet airs of our tun'd violins.[1]

The benevolent authority which King Charles sought to exercise over his people was reflected in many a noble and civilised achievement of the arts. With the help of courtier-landowners, inspired by the Crown, the embellishment of the capital proceeded apace. The piazza at Covent Garden, surrounded by splendid town houses for the nobility and dominated by the handsome new church of St. Paul, was all but finished. London's greater St. Paul's, the huge, decrepit medieval cathedral, had been purged of the hucksters who used the nave as a market place; the citizens who had for years tipped their rubbish into the crypt had been compelled to find another place for it. A magnificent portico in the Italian manner was being erected to beautify the outmoded Gothic façade.

The King's Surveyor General, the virtuoso Inigo Jones, had some admirable ideas for a new London, spacious, sweet and clean. London Bridge through the narrow arches of which, at high tide, the Thames flowed in dangerous rapids, was doomed to demolition; the crazy structure of houses surmounting it was grotesque and old fashioned, and for the last few years had become dangerous and unsightly owing to a fire which had left, on the north side, only burnt-out shells patched with boards. All this would soon be replaced by a stone structure, modelled on the bridge of Sant' Angelo in Rome, and worthy of a great capital and a great river. In the architectural schemes of Inigo Jones the new London already appeared to be, in outward form as it was in size, the greatest city in Europe.

In practice the King met with irritating opposition. When he decided to demolish the inferior little church of St. Gregory to free St. Paul's from surrounding clutter, the parishioners of St. Gregory sulked; they did not think their church inferior and they too had spent good money on improvements. Other more exasperating incidents interfered with the building of the capital. A fine vista had been planned in the suburban fields of Long Acre, but before work could be started on it, wooden hovels appeared overnight and by morning were full of clamouring squatters.

Apart from opposition there were the usual checks to which building operations are subject—bad weather, delays in delivery of material, mistaken plans which had to be rectified. The superb series of paintings commissioned by the King from Sir Peter Paul Rubens for the ceiling of his new banqueting house at Whitehall was ready more than a year before there was any ceiling to which to attach them. They had to be rolled up and stacked in the workshop of the master at Antwerp. When the ceiling was ready for them they were found to have cracked, and Rubens, who had put his highest efforts into their composition, had to devote some weeks' personal work to them before they were again ready for transportation to England. By the summer of 1637 they were at last safely in their appointed places, and revealed, to those who curiously or admiringly examined them, an allegorical tribute to the late King James of blessed memory.

At each corner symbolic groups illustrated the triumph of peace, wisdom and authority over strife, falsehood and faction: a serpent-headed Medusa writhed under the feet of her conqueror, and Hercules grappled successfully with the Hydra of rebellion. Along each side buxom children, who staggered beneath cornucopias or tumbled among garlands of flowers, conveyed the general idea of prosperity. The three great pictures in the centre showed the late King bestowing order, justice, peace and the benefits of true religion on his people, before mounting to heaven where a throng of Christian angels and pagan gods united to exchange his earthly crown for a celestial one.

In one of these pictures two ample nymphs representing the sister kingdoms of England and Scotland dandled between them a baby boy whose prancing legs and outstretched arms seemed to foretell at once the greatest energy and the noblest aspiration. This child portrayed King Charles himself as an infant. In prosaic fact, he had been a sickly little thing with no resemblance to the bouncing Flemish baby used by Rubens as a model, but the higher truth of allegory is not bound to pedantic details. The pictures illustrated the vision which both King Charles and his father had for their people—peace, order, justice.

A literal-minded critic might have found fault with the whole splendid composition of cloud-capped domes and sky-borne deities. These had little to do with the archipelago scattered out north-westward from the mainland of Europe, the British Isles, with their seven thousand miles of coast, towering crag and jagged reef battered by Atlantic storms, chalk ramparts above the green Channel, dune and quicksand, shelving shingle and crumbling cliff: the beacon on the headland, the bell on the rock, the fishing boats on the beach, the nets drying on the sea wall, the bales unloaded on the busy quays; and inland, the cornfields and the pastures, the sheep on the downs, the cattle in the hills, forest and park, moor and mine, impenetrable mountain and impassable bog; and the King's seven million subjects (more or less) crammed in towns, snug in villages, lonely in moorland farmstead or island croft; or far off on the rocky shore of Newfoundland, the wooded hills of Massachusetts, the warm islands of the Caribbean; or east or west on the world's wide oceans in some *Mary Rose* of Bristol, *Andrew* of Leith, *Patrick* of Galway.

All this was but vaguely comprehended in the vast allegorical design. The painter had not been asked, and had not been expected, to represent the geographical character of the King's dominions or the activities of his subjects. He had been asked to represent certain large and noble ideas, and he had, largely and nobly, acquitted himself of his task. It was not for him to reconcile the vision with the facts. That task fell to the King.

The races, customs, languages, religions and interests of the King's subjects were as various as the landscape of his dominions. The greater number of them lived in England which, with the adjoining principality of Wales, accounted for about five millions; Scotland and Ireland with the islands off their coasts had not above a million each.

A contemporary scholar reckoned that twelve languages were spoken in the British Isles. Only one of these, English, was officially recognised, and the aggressive, conquering language, now in its vigorous golden age, was bounded on the North and West by the older Celtic tongues, once the general speech of the land—moribund Cornish in the extremity of the western peninsula, lively lilting Welsh throughout the principality, and various forms of the melancholy, guttural Irish dialects in the Scottish Highlands, the Western Isles, the Isle of Man, and throughout Ireland. Norse dialects were spoken in the Orkney and Shetland Islands, French persisted in the Channel Islands and French or Dutch among the self-contained communities of refugees who had settled in the south and east coast towns during the last century.

The King's dominions were encircled and invaded by the sea. On the western littoral, jagged headlands and rocky cliffs fronted the stormy onslaught of the Atlantic ocean; on the eastern shores the sandy coastline slowly retreated before the pressure of the North Sea. The sea penetrated far into the interior, up the broad estuaries of Thames and Severn, Humber and Tyne, the Firths of Forth and Clyde and the narrow fjords of Loch Fyne, Loch Long, Loch Linnhe; it grasped whole handfuls from the Irish coast in wide bays and low-shored, labyrinthine loughs. In places the King's dominions were bogged and saturated by the sea, with acres of salt marsh, mud-flat and quicksand.

At least half the King's subjects derived their living directly or indirectly from the sea. Hundreds of fishing hamlets lay along his coasts. The delicacies and riches of the rocks and waters were eagerly sought. On the Cumbrian and Scottish shores the mussel beds yielded pale irregular pearls. The oysters of Colchester and Whitstable were famous; so were Selsey cockles and the shrimps of the sandy Lancashire shores. The Thames estuary had its teeming population of sprats and eels; eels, larger and richer, were the boast of northern Ireland, and lampreys were the speciality of the Severn estuary. Pilchards from Plymouth and Penzance were famous in far countries; mussels were the pride of Minehead. Plump sea-gulls were in demand, and the tiny, naked new-hatched gannet were carried away by the basket load from the Bass Rock to be swallowed, at one succulent, greasy mouthful, by revellers in Edinburgh. Berwick had long been famous for salmon and shellfish but had recently fallen upon evil times; the fisher folk, tempted by the possibility of a record haul, had broken the Sabbath and gone out in their boats. Since that time the salmon had deserted Berwick whose present distress was held up as a warning to all who despised the commandments.

From the North Sea the Yarmouth herring boats brought home by the barrel-load the silvery, living harvest of the deep, and fisher folk came in their cobles from as far north as the coast of Durham and as far west as Lyme to sell their herring on the Yarmouth quays to be split and smoked and marketed. From the ports of East Anglia—Lynn, Southwold, Dunwich, Aldeburgh—the Iceland ships went out for codling. On fish quays up and down the kingdom, housewives bargained for plaice and sole, cod and mackerel, turbot, skate, whiting and "poor John," as they familiarly called the vulgar hake, the Friday fare of the people. Sturgeon and whale, cast up on the coast, were for the King's use.

Far to the north the adventurous Scots were discovering the treasures of the Greenland whale fisheries, but the English Muscovy Company disputed the profitable fishing rights of the icy waters, and English money and resources weighted the scale against Scottish enterprise. Fishing rights in Scotland's own waters were savagely contested, for lowland intruders were opposed by the fierce people of the Highland coasts and the

Hebrides, and the aggressive Hollanders fell upon both alike.[2] Round the Orkney Islands the Dutch not only trespassed on the fishing but had, on occasion, fired on the poor coracles of the Orcadians, wilfully damaged the breeding grounds of their sea-birds, and plundered their villages.

Where the coasts were low-lying, hundreds of salt pans yielded the mineral wealth of the deep; refineries at Newcastle, Colchester and Chester perfected it. Where the coast was rocky, seaweed was carted inland to enrich the soil. On cliffs and sandhills men gathered samphire and sought for ambergris among the sea-drift on the shore, to sell to the kitchens of the rich. The river delicacies were also prized—fresh-water eels from Abingdon, Severn grayling, and Arundel mullet.

Thousands of small craft plied with goods and passengers from one little port to another. Stubby trows from Swansea carried the coal of South Wales across the Bristol Channel; Minehead and Barnstaple exchanged wares and travellers with Tenby and the ports of southern Ireland, Waterford, Wexford, Youghal, Kinsale and Cork. Fifty sail from these Irish ports would put into the Severn estuary for the Bristol fair in July, The small ships of Perth, Arbroath and Montrose connected the villages of Scotland's eastern seaboard better than the indifferent roads of the interior; those of Glasgow and Greenock linked the western Highlands with the Isles and Ireland. Hull, Yarmouth, King's Lynn, Ipswich and Harwich commanded England's east coast carrying trade. A fleet of three hundred ships carried New-castle coal to London. Dumbarton and Whitehaven sent colliers to Dublin, and the Irish Mail (wind and weather permitting) went from Chester. Ayr and Irvine traded to France; Leith, Dundee, Aberdeen and Stonehaven to Norway, Denmark and the Low Countries. A cross-Channel traffic from Dartmouth and Exeter brought in the flax and hemp of Normandy and Brittany and exported it again as sail cloth and buckram. Glou-cester, queenly among the meads of Severn, assembled the woolsacks of the Cotswold country for shipment to Bristol and beyond. Travellers for France took ship at Dover; for the Low Countries and Germany, at Harwich or from London.

From Bristol, Plymouth, Southampton ships set sail for the

Atlantic crossing with a hundred or two hundred men, women and children bound for the American colonies, and supplies of malt and meal, shirts and shoes, cloth and hardware for the settlers already there. Having discharged their cargo they turned northward, bought in Newfoundland fish, sold it two thousand miles away at Cadiz in Spain, and so came home again rich with Spanish wines.[3]

The King's subjects made a living from the sea in other ways besides fishing and merchandise. Lundy Island, the Orkneys, the Scilly Islands sheltered pirates; on the Hebrides, on the Blasket islands, on the Cornish coast and on the black, appalling cliffs of county Clare, delusive fires might burn by night to lure the lost vessel to the mercy of reefs and robbers. The great men of these parts, in return for a share in the profits of piracy and wrecking, would sometimes help their wilder neighbours and tenantry in deceiving and defying the government. A recent attempt to convert Stornoway into a more reputable port by settling merchant folk within it had been stubbornly defeated by the inhabitants. The depredations by sea and land of the Clan Macdonald had been fairly checked on the mainland of Scotland, but it was not two years since the *Susanna* of Limerick, driven against the coast of Lewis by a stormy sea, had been systematically plundered by the Macdonalds under one of their principal chieftains. Between northern Ireland and the Western Isles native coracles plied a traffic in crude liquor and fugitive criminals. They defied alike His Majesty's customs and His Majesty's justice, and preyed from time to time on the English-speaking settlers from London or the Scottish lowlands who were trying to turn the wild Ulster of the O'Neills and Macdonnells into a farming and flax-raising country.

Outside the great ports of the kingdom, foreign ships might be ill received. A Dutch ship damaged by Dunkirk pirates in the Channel had limped into Seaford for help and shelter, but the men of Seaford robbed the crew, ransacked the ship and stood at sulky defiance when the King's government commanded them to make good the damage. The inhabitants of Dunbar turned out with horses and wagons to carry off the cargo of a foreign ship that ran ashore a few miles from their town.

A Dutch East Indiaman, storm-driven into an Irish port, fore-
stalled any possible hostility by covering the place with its great
ordnance and landing a party to kidnap the son of its richest
citizen. The crew of another, which had taken refuge from
pirates in a remote Irish haven, terrorised the inhabitants, and
refused to pay customs on the goods sold to lighten the burden.
As the cargo was of spices, worth two hundred thousand pounds,
the King's Deputy in Dublin considered the possibility of
forcibly detaining and seizing it all, a design which was foiled
because this armed giant of the ocean was more than a match
for the English vessels sent to deal with it.[4]

Dunkirk pirates made English waters unsafe. The Barbary
corsairs raided the Devon and Cornish coasts and, repeatedly,
those of southern Ireland, so that the slave-markets of Africa
knew the fair-skinned boys and girls of Plymouth, Barnstaple
and Baltimore.

The King was enlarging his navy to protect his people. He
envisaged the addition of two major warships to his naval
strength every year, while experiments were being made with
a new type of ship, the small swift-sailing whelps. At Deptford,
where Drake's *Golden Hind* still lay at anchor slowly rotting,
crowds gathered to watch the amazing progress of the greatest
ship ever to be built in England. Still nameless, she rose majestic
in the stocks, while the best craftsmen in the country completed
the carving, the gilding and the paint which gave elegance and
richness to her formidable bulk.

The King's principal shipyards lay along the southern shore
of the Thames estuary. A few miles farther up the river, the
gigantic London and its satellite villages, the centre of maritime
and mercantile England, covered five miles of its northern and
three miles of its southern bank with houses, quays and towers.
Westward, the buildings ran out along the river bank as far as
Westminster; painted barges, cushioned and capacious, were
moored at the watergates of the great lords' houses that fringed
the Strand. Traffic came and went by water, bearing lawyers
to Westminster Hall and officials, servants, courtiers to the
King's sprawling palace-village of Whitehall. Eastward from
the Tower, the Ratcliff Highway joined Wapping, Shadwell

and Limehouse, mariners' villages looking out upon the great ships at anchor in the estuary, with green country and wind-mills at their backs; they brought in the produce of Essex, coarse hard cheeses and salted meat, to provision the outgoing ships. On the south bank, houses and quays were continuous through Rotherhithe and Southwark; thence they trailed away into the region of disreputable gaiety, the pleasure gardens and bear pits, theatres and puppet-shows and brothels of Bankside. A strip of marshland divided this district from the Archbishop's low-lying red-brick palace at Lambeth and the fields whence, on warm summer evenings, young Londoners went bathing. This great urban conglomerate numbered already close on a quarter of a million souls. In two wide half-circles, north and south, the outlying villages reached inwards to London, as London reached outwards towards them. They grew hay for London horses and vegetables for London tables; their windmills ground the corn for London bread and their innkeepers and dairymaids provided ale and cheesecakes, plums and cream for Londoners on holiday afternoons.

In the recently opened Hyde Park, on London's western perimeter, rich citizens strolled with courtiers and visiting gentry. The occupants of smart coaches showed themselves off in the Ring; there was horse racing and foot racing, two bowl-ing greens, a gaming house and an eating house, and dairymaids walked round with milk for the thirsty. For the humbler citizens of London, Finsbury fields were a favourite walking place al-though of late years much spoiled by the brick-works which supplied London's builders. Within the city itself Moorfields was set aside for citizens' wives and maids; here they could hang out their laundry or spread it on the grass; shady trees, specially planted, bore the names of those who had placed them there, and wooden shelters had been put up against sudden rain. It was pleasant by daylight but with nightfall it grew disreput-able, even dangerous.

London was first and foremost a seaport. The tidal river lapped at the streets' end; high masts and furled sails closed the narrow vistas of its ancient alleys. Greater than all the other seaports of the realm together, London was the mart of the known world. The Venetian envoy, who had experience in ships and shipping, reckoned that twenty thousand craft, small and great, were to be seen from London in a day. Rowing-boats and ferry-boats carried the citizens upstream and down, or from bank to bank; heavy barges distributed goods from London up river, and brought back to London the produce of the Thames valley. Merchantmen from Antwerp and Amsterdam, Calais and Bordeaux, Lisbon, Leghorn and Cadiz, Bergen, Hamburg and Archangel, Constantinople, the East and the West Indies, rode at anchor in the Pool or unloaded at the wharves. Some were privately owned, others belonged to trading companies— the Muscovy Company, the Levant Company, the West India Company and the Merchant Adventurers. Greatest of all towered the huge ships of the East India Company, "mobile, maritime fortresses" embattled against piracy and storm.[5]

London was a huge port and a huge town and, at its worst, as dark and wicked as such towns are. In the porch of St. Paul's, in the arcaded shopping centre of the New Exchange, the "coney catcher" loitered to ensnare some wide-eyed country rabbit with a little money in his foolish paws. The "jeering, cunning courtesan, the rooking, roaring boy" conspired to wheedle and bully unsuspecting fools. All day the shouts of oyster and tripe women, the swearing of draymen, the creak and clatter of hackney coaches dazed and deafened the newcomer, and after sunset

"riotous sinful plush and tell-tale spurs

Walk Fleet Street and the Strand, when the soft stirs

Of bawdy ruffled silks turn night to day."[6]

London was not a safe place for the innocent, although those accustomed to it, born in "the scent of Newcastle coal and the hearing of Bow bells," knew how to avoid the dangers, and the more experienced revellers who came in for a spree, like Sir Humphrey Mildmay who got home "mad, merry and late" after "playing the fool with two punks in a barge on the Thames," were very well able to take care of themselves.[7] But country boys and girls, driven to the capital by bad times or tempted by tales of easy money, drifted through disappointment and disaster into the criminal depths of the city, to die in the common gaol or of the "Tyburn ague" on the gallows.

As the town grew, and it was growing fast, its gaieties increased. Bear gardens and pleasure gardens spread along
Bankside, puppet-theatres showed *Bel and the Dragon* and other
apocryphal matter; peep-shows advertised *The Creation of the
World* represented to the life in pasteboard. The two principal
theatres, now both covered in and lit by wax candles, attracted
the rich and fashionable. Blackfriars successfully carried on the
Shakespeare-Burbage tradition, with Taylor, thought to be the
greatest Hamlet yet seen, and Swanston's much praised Othello;
the portly comedian Lowin played Falstaff and the whole
Jonsonian gallery of grotesques, and the fair youth Stephen
Hammerton drew tears with his Juliet and Desdemona. Christopher Beeston's company at the Cockpit in Drury Lane
concentrated on more modern topical works. These two had
the highest reputation though half a dozen lesser theatres, more
old-fashioned, open-roofed and playing by daylight, still drew
large audiences. A French company brought over the neo-
classical drama from Paris but the Londoners, taking it into
their heads to be scandalised at seeing women on the stage,
pelted them with rotten apples. The Queen, who patronised the
company, was indignant, and after a little the Londoners forgot
their moral views and accepted the novelty.

The tidal Thames, creeping into the heart of the city up
many an open inlet, ditch and hithe, did something to purify
the town. Fresh water had been brought within reach by the
New River Company which had diverted the river Lea to
Islington. But rosemary and jasmine were in constant demand to
disguise the putrid smells of streets and houses. London
children already suffered badly from rickets, and the various
epidemic diseases vaguely defined as plague caused ten thous-
and deaths in the bad year of 1636. In the following year, still
bad, there was something over three thousand victims.

The respectable citizens of London drew together against the
underworld of the criminal, the drunken, the defeated. Their
city might be one of the wickedest in Europe; it was also, as
a natural consequence, one of the most austerely pious. The
virtues of plain living and hard work were extolled and
practised; the Bible and the hundred churches stood firm against

the ballads and the playhouses. Religion was a fighting force in the city because it could never cease from fighting, "the miles between Hell and any place on earth being shorter than those between London and St. Albans."

Out of London and into London came and went carriers' carts by road and barges by water. The King's posts started for Edinburgh thrice weekly, but for the most part citizens relied on independent carriers and, except when they found it useful, looked with some resentment on government enterprise. Provincial carriers called at least once in the week, and sometimes more than once, at various London taverns; for Oxford and Northampton the carts left daily. The industrious John Taylor, doggerel poet, scribbler, traveller and busybody, had compiled a *Carriers' Cosmography* listing the available services, but his work had not been easy: the carriers had taken him at first for a government spy collecting information "to bring carriers under some new taxation."

For all heavier goods water-transport was generally esteemed better than the roads, which were rough at best, impassable in bad weather, and not free from thieves. The coastal boats loaded their cargo into barges in the reaches below London and the barges carried goods up the Thames to Reading and up the Lea to Ware. West coast shipping came into Gloucester whence the Severn barges carried the freight to Shrewsbury. The Yorkshire Ouse served northern Yorkshire, the Trent the midlands. The rivers, well-disposed by nature and assisted by the ingenuity of man, had made the English a relatively united and economically interdependent people. Water-transport could not link the wilder country of Wales and had not been exploited in Ireland. The rivers of Scotland, the rapid Forth, the headstrong Tay, the sandy silted Clyde, were beyond the control of seventeenth-century engineering. With few bridges, with troublesome fords often swollen by rain, they emphasised the divisions of Scotland. The elements of unity and prosperity were concentrated in England.

Next after the sea, the King's subjects drew their living from wool and all the industries surrounding it. They herded sheep on the Sussex and Wiltshire downs, in the rich pastures of Cotswold, in the Thames valley, on the Lancashire fells and the Lincolnshire and Yorkshire wolds, in the Scottish lowlands and the Welsh mountains. Wool towns had grown up wherever streams gave water-power enough to drive the mills which washed and whitened it. In manufacture the regions had their specialities. Scotland's plaids protected both highlanders and lowlanders against the rigours of the climate and were exported to all the colder regions of Europe; they were Scotland's principal export and worth more than all the rest together. Wales made coarse friezes, so did North Devon; Carmarthen specialised in flannel. Blankets from Witney in Oxfordshire were famous all over England. Bolton and Manchester wove the soft-textured woollens confusingly called cottons—confusingly because Manchester was already importing Smyrna cotton for her fustians and dimities. (Derby, Macclesfield, Leek and Nottingham, were abandoning wool for the manufacture of silk.) Bradford specialised in rugs and cushions; Kendal in Westmorland, Bewdley in Worcestershire, and Monmouth in the Welsh marches specialised in stockings and caps. Woodstock and Ilminster made gloves. The best cloth came mostly from the south, although Leeds and Halifax led the way for Yorkshire with fine broadcloth; in general, broadcloth was made round Reading and Newbury and in the Wiltshire towns. Wiltshire cloth was sold over all Europe, and some, shipped by enterprising city merchants to Ragusa, was marketed far within the dominions of the Turk. Coggeshall and Colchester were the centres of the coarse cloth manufacture—the baize and serges—of southern East Anglia; their wares went in bulk to religious houses abroad, and friars of Spain, Portugal and Italy were clothed by the Puritan weavers of Suffolk and Essex. Norwich, once the leading wool town of England, had lost its supremacy and was visibly declining. Gloucester was now, after the all-conquering London, queen of the wool trade strategically placed on the navigable Severn, linked by it to Shrewsbury where the fleeces of Wales were sold, and to Bristol the greatest outgoing port, after London, in the realm. Gloucester also drew to herself the famous fleeces of the white, square-bodied, long-necked Cotswold sheep, the greatest wool-bearers in the country.

York was for the north what Gloucester was for the west; and York claimed also to be what London was for the south. It was the northern centre for the exchange and distribution of raw wool and the finished cloth. But York was also the second capital of England, the seat of an Archbishop, the centre of the King's government in the north parts and, in its own opinion, in no way inferior and in many ways superior to London. Its magnificent walls, its lofty Minster, its forty churches, proclaimed a greatness which defied decline. While the King beautified London, his representative at York, the Lord President of the North, had majestically extended his official residence in the noblest European manner. It was rivalled by the mansion of a private gentleman, Sir Arthur Ingram, whose palatial Italianate house and garden were the wonder of the city. As for good fare York boasted that it could do better than London; northern appetites were hearty and "the ordinary in York would be a feast in London."

The making of cloth was, for the most part, a cottage industry. Women and children sat at their doors carding, spinning or knitting. In East Anglia the big windows of the cottages gave light to the looms which were the livelihood of the family. There were enterprises also on a larger scale, especially in Wiltshire and East Anglia. At Colchester a Dutch settler employed five hundred men and women, and was so hated by the independent weavers that, in a lean year, they burnt his mill.

The factory was not the only enemy of the English weaver. Merchants found it increasingly profitable to sell raw wool abroad, instead of finished cloth. Home fashions too were changing; boots were making long woollen hose superfluous, and linen caps were neater and more comfortable than woollen. Weavers, knitters, spinners everywhere, but especially in Essex, suffered the enforced idleness which brought want and hunger.

High in importance in his subjects' lives, after the sea and the sheep, was the mineral wealth of the King's dominions. In recent years the "Black Indies" of the Durham minefields had begun to yield their riches; coal was mined too in Lancashire, Derbyshire, South Wales and in southern Scotland, and surface workings were frequent over all the English midlands. Some of the northern mines were deep; one shaft went down three hundred feet, reputedly the deepest in Europe, and at Culross on the coast of Fife the workings ran far out under the sea. Coal was a principal export from Scotland, but in England coal was rapidly replacing wood as the favourite fuel, and little went abroad. It came by sea from Newcastle to London and thence by barge inland. At first it had been carried partly in vessels from the east coast ports and partly in London ships, but of late years Newcastle citizens had developed their own coal fleet of over three hundred vessels. With the rising demand for coal the Newcastle hostmen, as the middlemen who transported and shipped the fuel were called, had become rich and powerful. The London faggot-mongers, as their trade in wood declined, had tried to wrest the transport of the new fuel from the "Lords of Coal" in the north, but the King favoured Newcastle and contemplated granting the hostmen a monopoly of the transport. London, now warmed almost wholly by coal fires, envied the rising wealth of the black seaport in the north.[8]

While the quarrel between the transporters raged, the coal miners everywhere remained an outcast minority, a black, savage people living in hovels round the primitive workings. In Scotland men worked so unwillingly in the mines that the old principle of serfdom had been revived by statute in Fife, and the miners were held by law, from generation to generation, in a bondage whence there was no escape. Women and children helped the men, and in some places it was said that whole families camped underground from week's end to week's end, coming up only on the Sabbath for compulsory kirk. In both England and Scotland the absconding felon or homeless vagabond was liable to be forced into this despised and dangerous toil. The miners kept themselves apart from the rest of the population and retained, not unnaturally, terrible and diabolic beliefs. They worked with unprotected tallow candles, and none knew better than they the fearful things that the demons from Hell could do when they unloosed the fire hidden in the depths of the earth.

The miners who worked for metal were more respected,

although they too formed a class apart from their neighbours. Often, like the tin-miners of Cornwall, they lived under laws of their own. The lead mines of Mendip were worked by yeomen-miners; by the "custom of the hill" a man might stake his claim to his own small working wherever he struck lucky and set up his windlass. Lead workings pock-marked these hills for miles, causing roads to cave in and creating pitfalls for grazing cattle.

Copper was mined in Westmorland; copper, zinc and silver in the west country where German workers had been brought in by Queen Elizabeth. There were brass foundries near Bristol. King and Court entertained the highest hopes of the veins of silver opened up in South Wales by the indefatigable prospector Thomas Bushell.

Iron, after coal, was the chief mineral wealth of the country. It was a principal industry of Sussex and was worked also in Staffordshire, Derbyshire and Westmorland. Some doubt was felt about the workings in the Forest of Dean; as wood was still used for smelting the ore, the King feared that expansion of the iron works would destroy too much of the the forest. The forests of Sussex had already been consumed, and in Worcestershire they were fast disappearing because wood was needed for the salt refineries which had sprung up near the saline springs. Unlimited destruction of timber could not be allowed, English oak being of the first necessity for shipbuilding. Recent experiments in smelting with coal might, it was hoped, solve this critical problem.

English ironmongery lacked distinction. The coarse knives of Sheffield and the cheap swords of Birmingham were widely despised but widely used. The swordsmiths of Hounslow had a higher reputation, and Ripon was distinguished for the excellence of its spurs. A smear of black country ran right across south Staffordshire whose "iron men" returned the hostility and contempt with which the sheep-herding "moorlanders" of north Staffordshire looked upon them. Iron-working was a domestic industry given over to nails and pins, and families worked industriously each at its own small forge. In Staffordshire too there was a local pottery industry, conducted in the same humble domestic manner. But earthenware pitchers and

trenchers were not much used outside the clay regions; in
general, wooden trenchers and leather bottles were used by the
poorer sort, pewter by the better off. The finest harness and
leather work was made on the edge of the Cotswolds, at
Chipping Norton, or Burford, as famous for saddles as was
Woodstock for gloves.

The islands were well supplied with building stone. The
quarries of Scotland yielded granite. Marble was worked in
Derbyshire and northern Ireland, alabaster in Lincolnshire,
Staffordshire and on both sides of the Bristol Channel, at
Penarth and at Minehead. There were slate quarries in Wales,
Cornwall and Northampton. The Cotswolds had their own
beautiful limestone; Devon and Dorset mansions were built from
the fine yellow stone of Hamden Hill above Montacute. The
beautiful limestone from Portland in Dorset was coming into
fashion and black Irish marble was sometimes used for decoration: materials were brought from great distances to produce
a sophisticated and European style of architecture. But in much
English building local styles and materials still prevailed. Brick
was common for large buildings over most of the South although
in the North and West timber was much used. A conservative
people, the English retained Gothic details of decoration in
spite of cosmopolitan Renaissance influence, and English car-
penters showed remarkable skill in reproducing the ingenuity
of Gothic stonecarving in their decorative woodwork. Inigo
Jones, responding to the European fashion, denied to his workmen their individual fantasies; he—like the King in another
sphere—decreed that the single mind of the master-architect
should plan the entire building with all its ornaments. But outside the capital city medieval freedom of invention lingered yet;
the carved lintels of Worcestershire doorways and the plaster-
ornamentation of Essex and Suffolk houses displayed the simple,
gay imagination of the craftsmen who made them. While Inigo
Jones conceived of London as a sophisticated European city,
John Abell, master architect of Herefordshire, built the last and
largest masterpieces of the local style, the elaborate and ambitious timber town-halls of Hereford and Leominster. The
masons and builders of Scotland, by tradition and culture more

closely connected with Europe and especially with France, had brought to maturity a style in which Renaissance detail was combined with the asperities of the native manner. Turrets, lintels, and doorways, which recalled the softer landscape of the Loire, lightened the harsh architecture evolved in a cold climate and an unstable society, and carved staircases and painted walls and ceilings showed the taste of the richer and more modern lords and citizens.

England was rich in mineral springs, some of only local fame, others famous throughout the land. Bath was the oldest and, though much fallen from its Roman splendour, still a place of considerable resort for health and pleasure. Visitors could enjoy organised entertainments such as dancing and fencing matches, but the chief amusement was to watch the sick people, of all ages and sexes, stark naked but for linen caps, sitting immersed in the great bath. The younger spa, Tunbridge, which offered good public rooms and gaming tables, was temporarily the more fashionable; the fortunate visitor might see "six earls and lords in a morning at the Wells."

The saline springs of Droitwich and the medicinal waters of Buxton and Matlock were locally famous. Physicians spoke marvels of the waters at Knaresborough but they attracted the attention of the curious rather than the sick, because of their petrifying action.

Mining and manufacture notwithstanding, the King's dominions were still essentially rural. His people lived in small communities, were proud of local achievements, prejudiced in the local interest, and very close to the soil.

The countryside offered many simple delights. Izaak Walton and his companions could pass a summer's day in happy argument on the relative merits of their favourite sports, catch trout and chub in the clear streams, listen to the milkmaids singing and watch with tranquil interest the striped caterpillars on the leafy trees and the painted butterflies in the meadows. John Milton in one of his rare idle hours may have seen such dancing in the chequered shade as he attributed to "the upland hamlets." Girls as pretty if not as eloquent as Perdita gave out posies at the sheep-sheering. On winter evenings the young jigged and danced by firelight at Leap Candle or the Cushion Dance; all the year long they had their singing rounds and games, Sellenger's Round, John Come Kiss Me, and Barley Break. Rush-bearing ceremonies, blessing of cornfields and of springs, crowning the May Queen, roasting geese at Michaelmas and sucking pig at Lammas, varied the laborious year. Free beer flowed merrily at Whitsun-ales and harvest festivals, and boys in wigs and petticoats bounced about on hobby-horses to the uproarious delight of all. In strongly Protestant districts traditional Hallowe'en jollities were being ingeniously transferred to Gunpowder Treason Day on 5th November. But religious disapproval so far had had little effect on the celebrations which marked the end of August when London's Bartholomew Fair lasted close on a fortnight, and all over Lancashire and Somerset the wakes were held, usually in the churches, with dancing, drinking, pipe, tabor and fiddle. During the time of general holiday between Christmas and Twelfth Night a Lord of Misrule was still sometimes elected to preside over the festivities, and the old mockery of church ceremonies, permitted in medieval times, was occasionally indulged, but at greater peril. The King, when he came to hear of it, viewed with grave disapproval a swineherd's impersonation of an Anglican priest at a mock marriage. At all times of year, bridals and christenings were an excuse for merry-making and the distribution of gifts, garters, posies, ribbons and—if they could be afforded—gloves. In the lowlands of Scotland the poor people had thriftily invented the "penny bridal," an occasion when each guest paid his penny towards the day's revelling. As anyone could become a guest at such feasts, they were the occasion of noisy mirth, on which the respectable frowned and the Kirk made determined but unsuccessful war.

In the summer months picnic parties from the towns rode out into the country with baskets full of pasties, and London apprentices carried their girls to Islington, Tottenham and Hogsden for cheese cakes and cream. The rich and fashionable favoured the Three Pigeons at Brentford for week-end parties. The sports and pleasures of the gentlefolk were hawking and hunting, and bowls as they grew older; they matched their hawks and greyhounds against each other, and their horses at the local race meetings which were becoming regular events. Sometimes, as at Kiplingcotes in Yorkshire, a piece of plate was the reward of the winner. Newmarket and Epsom Downs were already famous, and horses, like Bay Tarrell, a Newmarket winner, and Toby, whose owner, a London merchant, had gilded his hoofs, were popular favourites. With racing went the bagpipes, and the winner was escorted through the crowds to their shrill music.

Travelling pedlars and mountebanks entertained the villages with their wares and their news; they performed simple operations, drew teeth, cut corns, lanced boils and successfully straightened wry-necked children by cutting the tendons. The crowder, or fiddler, ready to play for any festivity, the rope-dancer, the juggler, and the showman with a bear, or perhaps a monster, were popular figures in the villages and country towns. In Scotland a solitary camel, the King's property, was leased out to a warden who was permitted to show him off, by tuck of drum, at all times of day except during divine service.[9]

In their leisure time students and apprentices competed with the bow; village boys played ninepins, cudgels, or a rough kind of football. In some places local sports were annually held. The famous Cotswold Games, sponsored by jolly Captain Dover, took place every year on a broad-topped down that still bears his name. From miles around came men and boys to compete in running, wrestling, quarter staff and shooting, for a great distribution of prizes and favours. The enterprise enjoyed royal favour and aimed at creating a new Olympia. Several poets had celebrated it in rhyme.

The people had the free and spontaneous gaiety of those who live in the moment because the next may bring disaster. The happy lovers who in the summer embraced "between the acres of the rye," would in a famine-stricken winter cling together for warmth before a cold hearthstone. They enjoyed the good times, they endured the bad. Drought, frost, fire, flood were the enemies of all who lived by the land.

With the easy laughter and song went also a primitive delight in violence. Cock-fighting and bull- and bear-baiting were the sports of all classes when they could get to them, and a light-hearted squire like Sir Humphrey Mildmay in Essex would from time to time let out his bull to be baited by the village dogs. Cock-throwing, which meant pelting the poor birds with sticks or stones, was a traditional annual sport among village boys. The ducking of scolds, or leading them through the village bitted and bridled, and compelling their husbands to ride the pole were occasional village amusements. Domestic quarrels were violent in all classes of society; a London regulation forbade wife-beating after nine in the evening because of the noise. Gentlemen who were known to "fling cushions at one another's heads only in sport and for exercise" descended with ease from horse-play to fisticuffs; blows were exchanged on very small provocation and in the most unseemly places. The Murgatroyds, for instance, annoyed because another family walked into church ahead of them, knocked down and trampled on their rivals, causing a disturbance the echoes of which were several years dying away in the ecclesiastical courts.

The physical conditions of life were not easy for anyone. Few anodynes were known and none were effective; rich and poor alike suffered with little help all the varied torments of the flesh. Familiarity with pain bred, in all classes, a certain stoicism, a deep acceptance of suffering as part of the necessary order of the world and a willingness to inflict it and to see it inflicted.

The King's dominions differed greatly in the quality and character of their soil. In many regions, village communities still endeavoured to be self-supporting in necessities. Small crops of rye, barley and oats, beans and peas were sown in strips in the common field. Hogs pastured on the common or the beech mast in the woods, and were mostly slaughtered at Michaelmas when their lean flesh, smoked, provided the winter meat, and their bladders, blown up, made footballs for the winter's sport. Even in the Scottish Highlands the cattle-herding clans had their sparse crops of oats, sown and reaped by their women. Only in parts of Ireland nomadic communities still existed who scorned the plough and lived, year in and year out, on the milk and flesh of their cattle, such edible grasses and seaweeds as grew without their help, and, from time to time, the plunder of an English settler's barn.

The cattle-farming of the Celtic peoples in Scotland and Ireland survived from early times; their herds of lean and shaggy beasts had the freedom of the mountains and wilds. The Highland clans, ennobling the struggle for provender with the bloody romance of clan feuds, disputed their difficult country among themselves. No one else wanted it. But in Ireland, whose low-lying, spongy meadows provided good pasture, settlers from England and southern Scotland were thrusting the native people and their herds back into the bogs while they introduced better breeds of cattle and more economic methods.

Sheep-breeding in England had, for the time being, reached its utmost expansion. The towns which had fattened upon it had to be fed with other things than fleeces; experiments were made and methods discussed for increasing the yield of the earth, improving crops, developing wheat and barley in place of the cruder rye and oats. More and more land—for there was still much waste and forest land in England— was used for growing corn and raising cattle. Cattle for milk and meat and hides were being extensively bred in Devon and Somerset, in Herefordshire and the Midlands. The old complaint of the poor in the previous century that the sheep had eaten up the arable land was changed to a new one—that the cultivated land was eating up the common and the forest. The poor man needed the common and the forest so that he could collect firewood and pasture his hogs. Great landowners from time to time enclosed the waste land, but they were not the only encroachers. The yeoman and the labourer also made their surreptitious advances, and small hamlets grew up on the edge of forest and heath, the penurious outposts of landless squatters.

The regions had their specialities. The Sussex wheatear, a tiny bird, was praised as "a little lump of flying sugar equal to the best ortolans of France." In Kent acres of cherry trees provided a favourite fruit for London. In Herefordshire and Worcestershire, and in Somerset, especially about Taunton, and in Gloucestershire, "that rich and fruitful garden-shire",[10] the

far-spread apple orchards filled the autumn vats for cider.
Hampshire claimed the sweetest honey in the kingdom; so did
Bishop Auckland. Cheddar was famous for cheese, Banbury for
cheese and cakes, Tewkesbury for mustard, Pomfret and
Nottingham for licorice, and wide fields of crocus round Saffron
Walden explained its name. About London for twenty or thirty
miles the towns and villages were set in a chessboard of vegetable
gardens, cultivated in the Dutch manner, growing asparagus,
young green peas, cauliflower and carrots for the luxury market
of the capital.

The dairy produce of Devon was gaining reputation, and the
fat cattle of Herefordshire ambled along the drove roads, at a
comfortable rate of eight miles a day, to their doom in Smith-
field market. Northumberland boasted plump chickens and all
manner of poultry. There was not much to be said for Cumberland or Westmorland where travellers from the south were
shocked at the poverty and smallness of the hamlets, the bare
feet and uncouth accent of the people. Carlisle cathedral, to
the southerner, was nothing but "a great wild country church,"
and the city's aldermen wore blue bonnets, like roving Scots,
instead of felt or beaver hats. But game birds and venison were
plentiful in the north parts and "a huge standing water called
Windermere" produced a most delicious fish called a char.[11]

The poverty of Cumberland, which shocked southern travellers, was equalled by the poverty which met the English
traveller's eyes when he crossed the Border. Even in a gentleman's house flitches of bacon hung from the rafters in the
smoke of the best room, and the lady of the place did not always
wear stockings. The women of the one-roomed, turf-thatched,
mud-floored hovels wore their petticoats kilted above the knee,
but their feet and ankles were clean because they trod their
washing instead of handling it.

The best of Scotland was not on the Border. In Lothian,
cattle and sheep at pasture, and strips of oats and barley surrounded Edinburgh with an air of modest prosperity. The
stone-built capital of Scotland, wedged between rock and loch,
its tall forbidding tenements crowned by the airily graceful
lantern tower of St. Giles, was like no other town in the islands.

It was not, by any but Scottish standards, a rich town; the winds that whistled through its ravine streets blew upon marketing women shrouded in heavy plaids—the material of which, as an English traveller snobbishly remarked, his countrymen made saddle cloths. They were a hard-working, hard-headed people indifferent to outward appearances, very sure of themselves, independent and proud.

West from Edinburgh in the Lennox and in Clydesdale good mixed farming was to be found, orchard, corn and grazing land, fissured here and there with new workings of coal. The city of Glasgow which commanded at once its outlet to the sea and the system of roads, such as it was, that linked the south-west of Scotland had flourished considerably. It had as yet little reputation as a port, for the sandy Clyde was too shallow to take any but the smallest ships.

The region of Galloway was relatively prosperous because of the steady traffic that passed through its little ports for northern Ireland; it was also famous for sheep and mettlesome Galloway nags. Other regions of good farming, especially for barley and oats, were the carse of Gowrie, the gracious region between Perth and Montrose, and that strangely blest strip of land north of Cairn Gorm, fringing the northern sea, the "golden planure" of Moray. The cattle, deer and small wild animals of the Highlands, otters, badgers and ferocious martens, provided furs and hides which were a valuable export; even the skins of wolves which still roamed the wilder mountains had their price. Beyond the Highlands, the people of the more open northern lands of Ross and Caithness lived upon fish and cattle, a spare, hard existence which did not prevent the men of Caithness from being, in the opinion of the loquacious traveller William Lithgow, "the best and most bountiful Christmas keepers (the Greeks excepted) that ever I saw in the Christian world."[12]

In England and in the more fertile parts of Scotland intelligent farmers and landowners were considering ways of improving their methods and their land. In England the prevalence of common-field farming made large-scale experiments difficult, and in Scotland the system of land tenure, by which leases were terminable from year to year, discouraged long-term planning. But experiment was in the air. New crops and new methods were discussed by the educated. Potatoes and turnips were being tried but had not gained any popularity. Lucerne, clover and sainfoin had been suggested as possible crops to provide winter fodder for cattle, and thus make the wholesale slaughter of beasts every autumn unnecessary. But the ideas put forward by progressive theorists who wished to enclose all the common land and so curtail the spread of cattle diseases were highly unpopular. Occasionally a landowner like Sir Richard Weston at Sutton Place in Surrey conducted experiments in irrigation and the improvement of soil on a large scale. The King had given authority for the draining of some of the fen country, and a successful beginning had been made with Hatfield Chase, a water-logged region between Yorkshire and Lincolnshire which the Dutch engineer Vermuyden had reclaimed. But farmers complained that the local price of corn had gone down owing to the plentiful harvests from the new land.

Vermuyden was now reclaiming the fenlands round Ely, a scheme in which the Court was interested and into which the Earl of Bedford and a number of other distinguished shareholders had put large sums of money. This improvement, and others like it, was bitterly opposed by the fenmen who had long lived by fishing and fowling and had no inclination to see their hunting-grounds turned over to grazing:

For they do mean all fens to drain and water overmaster,
All will be dry and we must die, 'cause Essex calves want pasture. . . .
The feather'd fowls have wings to fly to other nations,
But we have no such things to help our transportations.
We must give place (oh grievous case) to horned beasts and cattle,
Except that we can all agree to drive them out by battle.[13]

The fenmen decided on battle. They assailed Vermuyden's workmen with showers of stones and repeatedly destroyed the works.

New manures, new methods of sowing and ploughing, the introduction of new domestic animals were also discussed.

Richard Childe, with some knowledge of the East, seriously considered the introduction of the elephant: a beast "very serviceable for carriage, fifteen men usually riding on his back together, and he is not chargeable to keep."[14]

New fruits and plants were assiduously cultivated by the rich. The King's gardener John Tradescant had introduced a small French willow tree, excellent for making baskets, as well as the merely ornamental acacia and lilac. His interesting botanical garden, recently opened at Lambeth, was rivalled by that created for the university of Oxford by Lord Danby. But experimental gardens, beautiful or medicinal, were being made everywhere; Sir Arthur Ingram's at York, ornamented with statues in the Italian manner, was famous and so was the fine garden of Moray House in Edinburgh. Many a country gentleman spent time and trouble introducing new fruits to his orchard and new flowers to his garden—the better kinds of apples and pears and such novelties as apricots, vines and raspberry canes, the Portugal quince, figs, melons, currants and damsons, walnuts, almonds and the edible chestnut. The flowering peach and laburnum were already popular, and Sir John Oglander in the Isle of Wight, recorded proudly in his diary that he had planted "in one knot all sorts of French flowers and tulips ... Some roots cost me 10d. a root."[15]

Neither the cultivation of their gardens nor wider schemes for reclaiming land could assuage the land hunger of the English or the lowland Scots. The Scots indeed had for generations now emigrated by families to the Baltic shores of North Germany and Poland, there to build up the Scottish–Baltic trade. The number of these foreign-dwelling Scots was estimated at nearly thirty thousand. But for new land both Scots and English looked towards Ireland. Scots and English intruders flourished in Ulster, English intruders in Munster; dairy farming had begun round Waterford and in Wicklow where English cattle had been introduced; good crops of rye and barley grew round Dublin; the government was encouraging the cultivation of flax for linen in Ulster; there was a growing export trade in Irish timber.

Another promised land awaited the adventurous on the

farther side of the Atlantic Ocean, where pioneers were planting their English cultivation and their English names—Plymouth, Taunton, Boston, Ipswich—on the shores of a gigantic unknown continent. Not very many of the King's subjects lived in this perilous land, in his opinion too far from his control: from Newfoundland to the Caribbean, not more than fifty thousand. For King Charles it sometimes seemed fifty thousand too many. If his people wanted more land, let them go to Ireland where he could watch over their religion, education and morals. The stream of adventurers went for other causes than the need for land alone; far from his paternal vigilance they practised uncouth religions and strange politics. He was considering whether it would not be wise to prohibit their going altogether.

The structure of society was still hierarchic, although with differences in the nature and the rigidity of the hierarchy in different regions. In England at the topmost level were noblemen of the old school who kept two hundred servants of all degrees, from their Master of the Horse and Gentleman Ushers, their Yeomen of the Buttery and Pantry, to laundresses and grooms, and who went on journeys with a trumpeter to give notice of their coming.[16] At the lowest level was the day labourer with one coarse shirt to his back, earning a night's lodging and a share of pease-pudding, and enjoying from time to time the free spectacle of the great lord and his train passing by. Great as was the distance between high and low, no insurmountable barriers separated, one from the other, the many ranks in between. There was unceasing movement up and down. A man might rise or sink by his own good fortune or his own endeavours. Gentility was to be acquired by intellect or valour or wealth; by English custom, all clergy, all university students, all lawyers and any man who had held command in an army might write himself down "gentleman", no matter who his father had been. In every generation tradesmen and yeomen made their way into the gentry not to mention the clerks and secretaries who rose by service to the great lords or the Court. The last step into the nobility was open to those who could pay the price for it either by direct purchase or by services to the Crown. The older nobility might look with contempt on these sons and grandsons of aldermen, financiers and clerks, these earls and barons who had paid cash down for their titles —Middlesex, Portland, Clare, Cork—but they received them in their houses and eagerly sought their daughters in marriage.

The downward movement was as persistent as the upward, and the feckless gentleman who wasted his estates could drop in a few years to the criminal depths of society. The attempt to save the situation by abducting an heiress was made more often than it succeeded. In the summer of 1637 Sarah Cox, a rich orphan of fourteen, was snatched from a party of schoolgirls walking on Newington common and carried away screaming by a young gentleman in a coach. Although she was forcibly married that day, her friends rescued her next morning, and her enterprising husband was thrown into prison.[17]

Love occasionally found a way and if the poor suitor won the lady's heart his chances were usually good. A city heiress, on the eve of her wedding to the dull husband of her guardian's choice, whispered to the handsome younger son of a poor Scots lord that "her affection was more to him, if his were so to her she would instantly go away with him." Receiving the necessary encouragement, she drove to Greenwich with him that night and married him.[18]

The nearness of the Court unsettled London wives and daughters. Courtiers had more persuasive manners than citizens, and the citizen's wife, showing off her new coach in the Ring at Hyde Park, might easily make a flattering conquest of some fine gentleman. An invitation to a Court masque or play might follow, and not all the excited young women who hurried to Whitehall in their best finery brought back an unsullied virtue to the paternal or conjugal hearth. "There is not a lobby nor chamber, if it could speak, but would verify this," declared a censorious writer. It was an insolent common boast of young courtiers that they had cuckolded half a dozen aldermen. In the City of London the moral reputation of the Court stood very low: the Queen was rumoured to be Harry Jermyn's mistress, or else Lord Holland's, nor was the King held blameless. These scandals were baseless, but jealous citizens repeated, magnified and believed them.

English women enjoyed unusual freedom; the tradition went far back and had much to do with the movement between class and class. When the Reformation closed the nunneries to the younger daughters of the rich or nobly born, they did not remain mewed up, unmarried, because there were no suitors good enough. They married where and how they could: the nobleman's younger daughter married the squire, the squire's younger daughter married the tradesman, the schoolmaster's or vicar's daughter might marry the yeoman, even the labourer, and so on to the lowest rungs of the social ladder. These women were a powerful, secret force, diffusing the pretensions and confidence of gentility in the humblest ranks of English society.

There was no legal and only a limited traditional objection to marriages which outraged the conventions. If the gentleman's daughter ran off with the footman her family might refuse to see her again but it was not an essential point of honour, as it would have been in some contemporary European countries, to wipe out the stain by killing the low-born seducer.

No English tradition prohibited gentlemen from following the professions or concerning themselves with trade. For the small squire it was nothing unusual to practise as a doctor or solicitor or to "get a ship and judiciously manage her."[19] Richer men adopted more ambitious courses. The powerful companies which financed colonial ventures and trade with Russia, Turkey and the East counted noblemen among their directors and shareholders. Many great families were already drawing their fortunes from coal and iron, not merely because these had been found on their lands but because they had themselves opened the mines and organised transport and marketing. The Willoughbies at Wollaton had started glass-furnaces to absorb the produce of the coal mines on their estates. The Byrons, on the strength of a rising fortune in coal, had become *entrepreneurs* and money-lenders on a large scale in the Midlands; the Robartes family, whose fortune was built on wool and tin, had done the same in Cornwall; the Ashburnhams were the largest iron masters in Sussex; the Lumleys financed the alum works at Hartlepool, and the Lambtons the salt refineries at Sunderland. Sir John Winter, of an ancient Roman Catholic family, leased the iron mines of the Forest of Dean from the King, and with the help of a cousin, Lord Herbert of Raglan a pioneer in experimental engineering, had greatly developed them. He had also acquired interests in the South Wales coal mines, and in the course of the next generation was to foreshadow that marriage between coal and iron from which, in good time, the Industrial Revolution would be born. The Lowthers in Cumberland were developing the mines of White-haven, linked with a fleet of ships to transport their produce to Ireland.

England had long since accepted the fusion of the feudal landowner with the industrialist and the merchant. The squire's younger sons were, in the order of things, apprenticed to trades unless their abilities fitted them for the law of the Church. Only the ardently adventurous or irremediably stupid were sent abroad with horse and arms to become soldiers in foreign service.

In all the larger towns, and above all in London, the short-haired apprentices who thronged about the place counted among their number gentlemen's sons, yeomen's sons, the sons of professional men and of citizens. There were distinctions between them of course; gentlemen's sons were naturally apprenticed to the wealthiest and most respectable men. The irascible master worked off his temper on the poor widow's son rather than the baronet's younger brother. But within the framework of the great corporations and before the laws of the city all were alike apprentices, and common interests, hopes and pleasures broke down the barriers of inheritance.

Instructive handbooks enabled the self-made to learn the manners and outlook of the class into which they had pene-trated. Richard Brathwaite's *The English Gentleman* and *The English Gentlewoman Drawn out to the Full Body* enjoyed con-siderable popularity. So did Henry Peacham's more ambitious *The Compleat Gentleman* which aimed at improving the ac-complishments of the gentry and instructed them in science, literature and art as well as fishing and heraldry. His *The Worth of a Peny* and *The Art of Living in London* were directed at the many young men who fell a prey to the cheats and temptations of the great city. The anonymous *A Precedent for Young Pen-men* instructed the uneducated, with numerous examples, in the art of polite letter-writing.

The movements and alliances between the classes did not prevent the careful observance of the differences between them; there would have been less point in climbing the social ladder had it been otherwise. None were more anxious to preserve the privileges of their order than those who had but recently risen to occupy it. The merchant who had married his daughter to a lord stood bare-headed in her presence until she gave him leave to cover. The citizen's coach made way for the knight's coach when they met in a narrow place. Relations who had come down in the world often entered the house of their more fortunate kinsfolk as servants and had no more than the rights of servants; the good-natured Ralph Josselin, a country vicar, recorded a generous resolution in his diary: "My sister Mary is come under my roof as a servant, but my respect is and shall be towards her as a sister."[20] Bowing, curtsying, taking off the hat, entering a room, sitting at table were all strictly regulated, although some conventions were declining, and old people grumbled at the free and easy manner of the young.

Some sports were for gentlemen only; special clothes belonged to certain professions. A labourer might play at ninepins but not at bowls, and his wife and daughter must wear petticoats and bodices as separate garments, not gowns like gentlewomen. Lord Stamford was indignant when a sporting vicar trespassed on his land with greyhound in leash and hawk on wrist and a hunting dress of a most uncanonical colour. A blacksmith's wife who ventured forth in a gown suitable to a merchant's wife was hooted back into the smithy by the people of Ludlow. But some conventions at least were growing slack. A petition had only recently been presented to the King praying him to prohibit the wearing of boots to the lower orders while there was yet time, for "divers inferior persons, both tradesmen and others ... wear boots as familiarly as any nobleman or gentleman, the which abuse doth not only consume much leather vainly but doth much hurt unto divers poor people which would have much employment by ... knitting of hose.''[21]

The family atmosphere of town and country life was declining but apprentices and sons still shared the house and table of the master and father, servants and family ate together in farmhouses, and in some parts of the country the honest labourer could still count on his Sunday dinner either at the squire's table or at that of a neighbouring farmer. Order of precedence was carefully preserved, and in a few houses the old phrase "below the salt" retained its actual and not merely its metaphorical meaning; the massive salt cellar divided masters from servants. But in the houses of the rich, by this time, separate tables or even separate rooms had become the custom.

Some great houses, particularly in the more rural North, retained the custom of piling the broken meats into tubs and setting them out for the poor, but fashions in food as well as fashions in living were bringing this medieval custom to its end. Foreign dainties, Italian sauces, "French kickshaws," as they were called, and the new elaborate ways of serving food with more emphasis on candied fruit and flowers, on elegance than on substance, were not suited to the old custom. Conservative writers already lamented the roast beef of old England as a thing of the past. Yet solidity had not wholly disappeared from a diet in which, for festive occasions, roast fawn stuffed with suet dumplings, boar's head with lemon, turkey stuffed with pheasant which was in turn stuffed with capon, made their appearance, and the autumn delicacy of all classes was the luscious sucking pig.

Local practice varied greatly, but such in the main was the structure of English society: a clearly defined hierarchy from landless labourer to nobleman, from unskilled journeyman to Mayor—but a hierarchy without barriers, a steep ladder on which men and women passed continually up and down.

This situation was not reproduced in the adjoining lands. The gentry of Wales were as a rule poorer and simpler than the

gentry of England. "You can sooner find fifty gentlemen of
£100 a year than five of £500," recorded an observer from England, or, as a traditional jingle put it of one Welsh county:

> Alas, alas, poor Radnorshire,
> Never a park, nor ever a deer,
> Nor ever a squire of five hundred a year
> Save Sir Richard Fowler of Abbey Cwm Hir.[22]

But the Welsh gentleman in his stone-built farmhouse, with
salmon hanging in the smoke of his chimney, a dresser with
wooden trenchers upon it, fixed benches round the fire and
about the walls, and a woven cloth for the parlour table on a
Sunday, lived a traditional and patriarchal life among servants
and tenantry who looked upon him as something more than
employer and landlord and felt for him and his a tribal loyalty
and pride. Often he still did not trouble himself to have an
English surname; knowing well by oral tradition that he was
descended from royal stock, he scorned the English insistence
on family names; himself he was David Evans; his son, called
Evan from his grandfather, would be Evan Davis. His life,
impoverished reflection of the Celtic tradition, had a simplicity
and poetry of its own, but even in its decadence Celtic society
was more rigid than the competitive, make-your-own-way
society of England.

Ambitious Welsh boys sought their fortunes not at home
but in England, where their alert faces, quick tempers and
musical accent were teasingly accepted. Eloquence and imagination often carried them far in the church or in the law; John
Williams, Bishop of Lincoln, was only the most remarkable of
the many Welsh bishops in the British Isles, and two of the
King's twelve Judges, John Trevor and William Jones, were
Welshmen. Some of these distinguished Welshmen would come
home in mature years, settle benevolently among their poor
countrymen, patronise and encourage local talent and offer the
wealth and fame won in England to swell the diminished glories
of their native Wales. More often the emigrant Welsh, successful or unsuccessful, stayed in their adopted country, and the
names of Jones and Trevor, Vaughan, Evans and Morgan

would be found, sparsely, in parish registers over all the English midlands, the south and west.

In Wales itself the poverty of the people and the patriarchal structure of society made it possible for a few great landowners to wield immense influence and power—families like that of Herbert, carrying half a dozen titles, or Somerset, whose head, the Earl of Worcester, lived at Raglan. Here in Wales the old feudal system superimposed four centuries earlier on the Celtic world had persisted, strengthened by the profound loyalties, rivalries and hatreds of the Celtic tradition.

In Scotland, where the Celtic world, hostile and unsubdued, had been penned into the Highlands, the situation was unlike that in Wales and England. Lowland Scotland, predominantly Anglo-Saxon in race and English in speech, kept perpetual watch on the untamed Highlands, but the feudal organisation imposed on this southern region in the twelfth century had acquired a patriarchal quality from contact with the Celt. The King himself in Scotland was not—as in England—regarded as the feudal overlord and fountain of justice and authority; he was regarded patriarchally as the head of the family. He was King of *Scots* not of Scotland, a ruler with a personal relationship to his people.

The Scottish laird, simply clad in homespun, with his blue bonnet on his head, ruled among his tenantry and servants with the intimacy, affection and arbitrariness of a father. He kept open house for travellers; he relieved the poor at his gate; his people called him by the name of his estate and he called them by the names of their farms. This gave a deceptively friendly air to a relationship which was dictatorial and could be tyrannous. The tenant Scots held their land upon annual lease, and the landlord who found minerals upon his estate, as many now did, might reduce his dependent farmers to landless men overnight at the year's end. The lowland Scots were discovering the mineral wealth of their country and developing shipping and trade of all kinds; compared to England theirs was a harsh and difficult world, where economy and stubborn toil alone yielded rewards. The belief that the Lord had His Chosen

People and rewarded them, gave a terrible intensity to Scotland's struggle to establish herself in the pattern of European economics, with her wool, coal, timber and fur exports and her fisheries. The Lord placed coal mines upon the lands of His Chosen; since theirs was the earth and the fulness thereof, it was clear that those who were dispossessed, or forced down the mines in the process, were none of the Lord's people. The belief was not cynical; it was often associated with a strenuousness of austerity and prayer that showed—if in a strange fashion—a deep sense of gratitude and responsibility for the Lord's well-placed gifts.

In the highlands the Celtic clan system generally prevailed, although the ancient clan loyalties were here and there crossed by feudal conceptions of land tenure. The Mackintosh, for instance, was accepted as chief in districts which, by feudal tenure belonged to Huntly, chief of the Gordons. Conversely he was feudal overlord of other regions inhabited by the Cameron clan. This confusion of rights was fruitful of trouble in a land where clan chiefs still in practice had rights of life and death over their people; whatever laws the Crown might pass to curtail this jurisdiction, such men as Argyll, Huntly, Seaforth had a moral and actual power over Campbells, Gordons, Mackenzies which extended to every part of their lives. Among themselves the highlanders were tenacious of their enmities: Campbell slew Macdonald, and Macdonald Campbell whenever they could. The Mackenzies were at feud with the MacLeods, the Gordons with the Crichtons, and every man's hand was against the MacGregors and MacNabs. The land was terrible and bloody, but with a wild beauty dear to those who knew it. In the late summer the clans gathered for the hunting; lesser quarrels were temporarily at rest while for long days over the great hills, they encircled and drove the deer. Sometimes, in the summer days the young men camped together in the meadow land by Tay or Spey, enjoyed the season's sport, swam, wrestled, leaped, danced, through the warm nights when dawn came after sunset with scarce a resting time between. In highland games or highland wars, the sons of the greater chiefs, who had been at the French Court or the English and had learnt the delicacies and graces of cosmopolitan civilisation, slept on the ground among their clansmen, wore—with a cultured elegance—the plaid and trews of their native land, spoke Gaelic, listened to the interminable songs of bards and the sharp music of the pipes, and watched the sword dances and the revels by the long sunset light and the glow of the turf fires.

Some of the southern nobility came north for the hunting; those whose lands lay along the highland frontier—Montrose, Ogilvy, Mar, Eglinton—were usually present. These had adopted some of the highland ways, probably "had the Gaelic," sometimes called themselves chiefs although they were in effect merely heads of families. Their function in the strategy of Scotland was to prevent highland incursions into the richer lands of the South, but over centuries of strife they had learnt to admire and imitate the very things they fought. Sometimes too a foreign visitor was welcomed to the highland hunting; an intruding cockney John Taylor, clad in a kilt lent him by the Earl of Mar, squatted on the unfamiliar, uncomfortable ground throughout the weird dances and wondered why these extraordinary people did not cut down their pine forests and trade them as masts to the shipyards of the world.

Between lowlands and highlands an armed neutrality reigned, broken from time to time by cattle-raiding. The highlanders, who knew that the land had been all theirs until the Saxon came, esteemed it no robbery to steal back something of their own. Lawlessness of the same kind prevailed on the English border. The late King James, when he succeeded to the English throne, had tried to pacify the borders with a strong hand, and for a time his armed patrols, his hangings and deportations of the border reivers, Scots and English, had brought an illusory calm. But the tradition of valiant robbery and lawlessness was too strong to die in a few years. Under the relaxed vigilance which marked King Charles's reign, the borders had gone back to their old way of life and by 1635 great parts of the country were terrorised by armed gangs who lived by robbery, kidnapping and ransom and revenged themselves so horribly on any who informed against them that few dared do so. The treacherous slaughter of the Laird of Troughend, the subject of one of

the finest of the border ballads, was a part of this tale of blackmail and vengeance.

In Scotland the Celtic North and the Anglo-Saxon South were
separated by the geographical divisions of highlands and lowlands. No division so convenient existed in Ireland where alien
invaders from England had forcibly thrust themselves upon an
angry Celtic land. The first settlers, the Normans, had become
in the course of centuries acceptable to the Irish chiefs. The
great family of Butler—Earls of Ormonde—were cross-bred with
Irish families; so were the Fitzgeralds and the de Burghs commonly called Burke.

In the last seventy years new settlers had descended upon
Ireland, first from England, then from the lowlands of Scotland.
These were calculating, adventurous, competitive, bent on
developing the latent possibilities of an undeveloped land, and
Protestant, with a Protestant government behind them. The
wild Irish were as alien to them as the American Indians to the
settlers across the Atlantic. Against these pushful newcomers,
the Irish and the Norman-Irish drew together—aristocrats, with
their retainers and their clans, a patriarchal society against
upstarts.

Apparent peace prevailed, and the royal government, as
represented by Lord Deputy Wentworth, hopefully cherished
the ambition of seeing Ireland "enclosed and husbanded, beautified with towns and buildings and stored with an industrious
well-conditioned people." Dublin at least had been improved
with handsome modern additions to the Castle, a pleasant meeting place for coaches and equestrians at Phoenix Park, and a
theatre for which the fashionable James Shirley had written the
opening play. The Deputy ostentatiously placed his own son at
Trinity College (which Queen Elizabeth had founded) as an
encouragement to other distinguished residents to do the same.
Under government patronage Christopher Syms had composed
a new Latin grammar specially designed for use in Irish schools
and published recently in Dublin.

Appearances were deceptive. The Irish retained their religion and their unconquered independence of spirit. Their clans
remained loyal to their chieftains, whether these were exiles

far away, like the Red O'Neill, or friendly to the English government, like Randall MacDonnell, Earl of Antrim, or Murrough O'Brien, Earl of Inchiquin, chiefs respectively of the largest clans in the north and south. Scattered nomadic hordes still lived in the shelter of the hills and bogs, levying blackmail on their neighbours and raiding the settlers when they dared. The worst danger was not from them but from the covert hostility of an entire population. Here in Ireland, sooner than any thought or feared, the struggle of eleven hundred years between the Saxon and the Celt was to burst into a new and terrible blaze.

The same clash of ideas and interests was reproduced in miniature midway between the Irish and the English shores on the Isle of Man. Twelve miles across and thirty-three miles in length, it belonged to Lord Strange, the Earl of Derby's eldest son. He found its lively, loquacious inhabitants faithful to their old customs in spite of benevolent attempts to bring their peculiar system of land tenure into line with that of his other possessions on the English mainland, and to reform their laws. The greatest native family was that of Christian. Its present head was especially powerful because of his many sons; illegitimacy mattered little among the Manxmen and the head of the Christian family bore patriarchal sway over his people. His opposition compelled Lord Strange to modify his policy; for the time being he had accepted Captain Christian as Dempster, which meant that he virtually ruled the island in Lord Strange's name.

The Celtic populations were a significant and possibly a dangerous minority in the King's dominions. They represented an antique challenge to the modern world in a way that the French-speaking Channel Islanders and occasional groups of foreign refugees did not. At the moment, the Channel Islanders were resentfully and jealously guarding their ancient privileges against government encroachment, but they shared with the English and the Lowland Scots much the same outlook on society and the world, although they might have lesser differences of interest and opinion.

Another kind of society, secret and submerged, persisted in

the King's dominions: the gypsies. They were known to the people as wanderers and vagabonds, distinguished from the ordinary vagabonds and thieves who roamed the country by a peculiar language and a closer organisation. Ballads occasionally romanticised them but the law persecuted them, and in the lowlands of Scotland to be a gypsy might in itself prove a capital offence.

Such were the peoples over whom King Charles reigned, and to whom he wished to give the blessings of peace, justice, order and true religion, under the unquestioned authority of the Crown. The ideal was constantly before his eyes but the intellectual and aesthetic fashion of the day, strongly bent towards allegory, obscured the practical difficulties of the task. The King lived in a world of poetic illusions and could not but be affected by them. For him and his courtiers, the most ordinary events were swiftly wreathed in pastoral or classical disguise. The Countess of Anglesey gave an evening party for the Queen and at once the poets summoned the goddess Diana and bade the stars shoot from their spheres;[23] Lord Bridgewater's three children made a long journey, and Comus with all his rout sprang eloquently forth to provide a masque and a moral to celebrate their reunion with their parents.

A young poet, hailing a new arrival at Court, cried out:

> "What's she, so late from Penshurst come,
> More gorgeous than the mid-day sun
> That all the world amazes?
> Sure 'tis some angel from above,
> Or 'tis the Cyprian Queen of Love
> Attended by the Graces."[24]

But it was only the Lady Dorothy Sidney with the usual duenna and waiting women.

Arcadian scenes were rhymed and sung, with splendid or with humble staging, in many a school or college hall or private house. Almost every year the King himself acted in a Christmas masque, and, recently, the most expensive masque ever mounted —it cost over £20,000—had been put on in his honour by the lawyers of the Inns of Court. It had represented the Triumph of Peace, and the masquers, about two hundred of them, had

ridden through the streets of London by torchlight in the quaint
and gorgeous finery designed for them by Inigo Jones.

The King had approved of this masque, written by the skilful and much favoured James Shirley. It too had enacted that
same allegory which he had commissioned Rubens to portray.
Peace, Law and Justice had, with song and dance, triumphed
over folly, faction and idle criticism.

The allegorical trick in poetry and compliment insensibly
spreads to other things and becomes almost a habit of mind.
The King seemed sometimes to treat administration and politics
as though the peace and contentment of the realm were indeed
assured because, at his Christmas revels, a golden chariot upon
a white cloud had descended against the heavenly backcloth
bearing Peace, "in a flowery vesture like the Spring," with
buskins of green taffeta, a garland of olives on her head and a
branch of palm in her hand.[25]

King Charles had been nourished from childhood in a deep
understanding of the sanctity and responsibility of the sovereign's part. His father, long since, had written a book, *Basilicon
Doron,* a short impressive manual on the duties of a King,
intended for the instruction of his eldest son; that eldest son,
Prince Henry, had died, and the younger boy, then his father's
cherished Baby Charles, had inherited, along with all else that
would have been his brother's, the wisdom and policy enshrined
in this book. He must, as a boy, have carefully turned over on
his stammering tongue and conscientiously pondered in his
mind such sentences as these:

> [A good King] acknowledgeth himself ordained for his
> people, having received from God a burden of government,
> whereof he must be countable.

His father, in this book, repeatedly emphasised that the relationship between King and people is that of a father to his children,
and that his authority, like that of a father, is founded in the
immutable decree of the Almighty. Just as no misconduct on
the part of a father can free his children from obedience to the
fifth commandment, so no misgovernment on the part of a
King can release his subjects from their allegiance. But the
King, like the father, has duties and must answer to God if he

scants them. This, in essence, was the doctrine of Divine Right as digested and set out by the late King James and as it had been imprinted on the mind of his son. Other writings by the old King were extant, and these too had been studied by the young Charles. "A good King will frame his actions to be according to the law," he had written in his tract on *The True Law of Free Monarchies,* "yet he is not bound thereto but of his good will." In fact it lay with the King to keep or break, make or unmake the laws. In his *Defence of the Right of Kings,* provoked by the rise of certain impertinent theories of popular and clerical rights against the Crown, he had declared:

"My brother princes and myself, whom God hath advanced upon the throne of Sovereign Majesty and supreme dignity, do hold the royal dignity of His Majesty alone, to whose service, as a most humble homager and vassal, I consecrate all the glory, honour, splendour and lustre of my earthly Kingdom."

With a profound sense of his holy office, therefore, and a deep conscientiousness, the earnest and self-disciplined Charles had taken up the burden of kingship, in the early hours of 27th March, 1625, when it pleased Almighty God to call King James to Himself. He was twenty-four. At his coronation he had defied tradition. He had refused to make the solemn rite an occasion for vulgar display and had omitted the customary procession, so popular with Londoners. He had also carefully revised the coronation oath in accordance with his views, swearing to maintain the liberties and laws of the country only in so far as they did not clash with his prerogative. He had eschewed as far as possible the pompous trappings of royalty and had worn white for his consecration. The text chosen for the sermon—it aroused some comment at the time—was *Be Thou faithful unto death and I will give thee a Crown of Life.*

The King's ideals were clear from the first. He wanted his subjects throughout his dominions to accept his absolute authority with unquestioning obedience and to belong with uniform and regular devotion to the Church established by law. This was the only just basis of government as he saw it; this once achieved he would—*of his good will,* and not by any legal obligation—protect their traditional rights and freedoms within the framework of the laws, and ensure equal justice, order, and as far as in him lay, prosperity and security to his good people.

No ruler can pursue an effective policy at home or abroad without money, and the revenues of the Crown were inadequate. It lay with Parliament to vote money to the sovereign, and the King had found, within a few months of his accession, that Parliament was very far from accepting his view that it existed and functioned only by his good will. In the first five years of his reign he had quarrelled with three Parliaments in succession. In 1629 he had got rid of the third, in spite of a violent attempt on the part of his principal opponents to prevent the dissolution. He had committed the leaders of the tumult to prison without trial, made peace abroad, and settled down to conduct his own affairs in his own way.

The King had shelved his problems, not solved them, and the beauty and order with which he had surrounded himself deceived him into the belief that his authority in his kingdoms was as absolute as his authority at Court. He turned away from less pleasing realities, contemplated with pardonable satisfaction his beautiful palaces, his well-behaved Court, his bishops and chaplains, and took this seemly shining surface to indicate an untroubled deep.

His Court reflected his own personality and ideals. He never criticised his father, but he had early perceived the incongruity of King James's theory of monarchy with the jovial squalor in which he chose to live. In his most impressionable years, the young Charles had been for many months at the Court of Spain, wooing the Infanta. The wooing had come to nothing but he had brought back from Spain the memory and the knowledge of a Court ceremonial after his own heart. On his accession the broad Scots jokes and the drunken romps which had amused his father abruptly ceased. Babbling quarrels in ante-room and corridor were stilled. From the Gentlemen of the Bedchamber to the waiters at the sideboard, each man precisely knew where to be and when, at which table to take meat, when to attend prayers, when the King would rise, when sleep, when ride, when give audience, and who, with staff of office in hand or napkin on arm, should walk before him or stand behind his chair. The formality of the Court on all official occasions was rigorous and extreme. The King, alone of European princes, was served on bended knee, and when the French ambassador complained because neither chair nor stool was set for his wife —as was done for the English ambassador's wife in France— he was told that on official occasions no lady of the English Court except the Queen herself, not even the Princess Royal, was allowed to sit in the royal presence.[26] King Charles lived, with no vulgar ostentation, but with elegance and ceremony.

The reform was partial only and did not extend beyond the King's immediate circle. The rabbit-warren palace of Whitehall was a village in itself; in its streets, alleys and outbuildings, a crowded world of dependants, professional courtiers, servants' families and servants' servants lived parasitically on the Court. The Venetian envoy, considering the King's surroundings with a critical mind, condemned his housekeeping as extravagant.[27]

The disorders of such hangers-on were not before the King's eye. He ruled his immediate surroundings with an absolute authority. Had it not been for the licensed gaiety of his French Queen, the Court would have been intolerably strict. She, who loved dancing, masquing, plays and music, enlivened Whitehall and Hampton Court with elegant and innocent frolic. Not only did she and the King take part in the Christmas masques and often bring professional players to Court to perform for royal birthdays or Twelfth Night revels, but she herself, breaking all precedent, had been known to attend public performances at the theatre in person.

The wilder young courtiers looked for additional pleasure, far from the restraint of their monarch's presence; they frequented the gaming tables of Piccadilly, the race course of Hyde Park, the taverns of Westminster and the Strand with their legal or literary gossip, or the expensive, disreputable pleasure gardens south of the river, where, it was said, a single supper with Bess Broughton, or her like, might stand a man in twenty pounds, not to mention what the lady's favours would cost him. But the Court remained, none the less, the focal point of society and the ultimate standard of taste and manners.

It was also an intellectual centre, the meeting place of talent and wit, not less than fashion and beauty. The poets and writers gathered in the gardens of St. James's and Whitehall or the Queen's drawing-room at Somerset House; here they neatly turned their *vers de société* or circulated prose *Characters* and satirical epigrams to amuse the ladies. Suckling risked the mischievous innuendo, Lovelace was frivolous and musical, Davenant musical and courtly. Less talented courtiers with pretensions to poetic gifts circulated their work anonymously and were often mortified at its reception.

The courtiers' talent spilled over into the life of the capital when they turned to drama and mounted their own plays at the London theatres, often with great splendour. The King, as patron, critic and censor, sometimes intervened: he persuaded Suckling to change a tragic to a happy ending, and, with a surprising realism, he discouraged his master of the revels, Sir Henry Herbert, from removing the realistic expletives from the dialogue of Davenant's social comedy, *The Wits*.

The King cultivated music more than poetry; his small private orchestra entertained him as he sat at meat with choice pieces of secular music or, in the Chapel Royal, performed delicate and complex sacred airs, to the scandal of some of his subjects who thought that God's house was no place for Italian fiddlers.

The King's greatest achievement was the superb collection of works of art which he had been accumulating since he was Prince of Wales. Rubens himself had described him as *"le prince le plus amateur de la peinture qui soit au monde."* His own excellent taste and the advice and gifts of intelligent agents had enabled him to fill his palaces with the rarest and the greatest collection in Europe. He possessed antique marbles and Florentine bronzes, delicate ivories, cut crystal, and the most rich and curious work of the goldsmith and medallist. Many of the noblest works of the Italian masters hung upon his walls—Titian's great "Entombment," Mantegna's incomparable "Triumph of Julius Caesar," Tintoretto's "Nine Muses," white-limbed on a sun-dappled Parnassus, Correggio's "Marriage of Saint Catherine," portraits by Raphael, allegories by

Giorgione; the works of the Bassano and Carracci families, of Giulio Romano and the younger Palma filled the gaps. Of contemporary artists, he commissioned paintings from Rubens and possessed those of Rembrandt; he employed in work for his Court and collections Anthony Van Dyck, Daniel Mytens, Gerard Honthorst, Wenceslas Hollar, Francis Klein, the ageing Italian master Orazio Gentileschi with his talented daughter Artemisia; Balthasar Gerbier, miniaturist, architect and indefatigable busybody of the studio and sale room, assisted and advised him, and he had secured for the chief artist at the mint, the skilled French engraver Briot.

He had bought the magnificent cartoons drawn by Raphael for the Vatican tapestries and sent them to the English tapestry works at Mortlake to be copied, while he commissioned Van Dyck to design appropriate borders for the woven pictures. He had also given encouragement to the Mortlake works by commissioning great numbers of hangings for his palaces. In spite of all, the works had got into difficulties, and Charles, with some idea of making the industry a royal monopoly, bought them for the Crown.[28]

The fashion in tapestries, pictures, and classical decoration set by the King in his palaces at Whitehall, Greenwich, Oatlands and Hampton Court was followed by his nobility and courtiers. Lord Arundel's house was rich in Italian marbles; Lord Pembroke had the famous double-cube room at Wilton decorated by Van Dyck; the splendours of the Marquis of Winchester's Basing House were legendary; at Ham House the King's friend Will Murray had ceiling and wall decorations in paint and plaster work of great elaboration, some of them copied from the architecture depicted in the Raphael cartoons his master had bought.

Although the arts were his chief delight the King respected and encouraged the sciences. The physicians who enjoyed the honour of his patronage included pioneers of the new learning like Sir Theodore de Mayerne, the great exponent of clinical medicine who had probably saved the Queen's life at the premature birth of her first child, and William Harvey, the discoverer of the circulation of the blood.

The numerous lords and gentlemen who meddled with scientific and mechanical matters also felt the attraction and solicited the patronage of the Court, partly, but not exclusively, in the hope of acquiring profitable patents for their inventions. Lord Herbert of Cherbury had rooms in the royal palace to give him easier access to the papers he needed for his projected work on the life of Henry VIII; in the intervals of history he solicited the King's attention for various practical inventions of his own —gun-carriages, naval equipment, and a floating bathing establishment to be installed on the Thames. The talented son of the old Earl of Worcester, Edward Somerset, devoted his ingenuity to water pumps and hydraulic lifts for his father's castle at Raglan on the Welsh border, but when business brought him to Whitehall he gained the intelligent approbation of the King. Sir Francis Kynaston, courtier and poet, secured the King's patronage for a school that he founded for young noblemen, but was less fortunate in getting him to adopt a new kind of furnace for use in warships. Charles Cavendish, the Earl of Newcastle's brother, an amateur mathematician who was in touch with many foreign scholars, doubtless had the King's approbation in his several attemps to persuade the French mathematician Claude Mydorge and the French philosopher René Descartes to make peaceful England their permanent home.[29]

The English Court was the abode of ceremony, elegance and learning. It was also the abode of beauty. The noble ladies in silks of pale saffron and coral pink, sky-blue, willow-green and oyster, their ringleted hair framing plump, oval faces, went by water to Blackfriars and had their likenesses recorded by Anthony Van Dyck: Lucy, Countess of Carlisle, bold and handsome; Lady Ann Carr, pensive, dangling her gloves; Lady Mary Villiers, with palm and lamb as Saint Agnes.

The courtiers were depicted in masque attire, nonchalant in buskins with a shepherd's crook like Lord d'Aubigny, or with appropriate accessories—curly-headed George Digby, Lord Bristol's scholar son, with papers and a globe, the connoisseur Lord Arundel with a choice marble statue, Algernon, Earl of Northumberland, Lord High Admiral of the Kingdom, with an anchor and a naval battle behind him, Viscount Wentworth, the Lord Deputy of Ireland, with one of the huge Irish wolf-hounds which he bred at his hunting lodge near Dublin.

The smaller luxuries which surrounded these men and women have been etched in loving detail by Wenceslas Hollar, the Bohemian drawing master of the King's children: the lace collars and cuffs, the knots of satin ribbon, the fur muffs, the painted fans, the embroidered gloves, the jewelled hat-bands and silver shoe-roses, the fringed velvet and tiffany masks to shield their waxen skins from wind and sun.

The small, fastidious King presided fittingly over his well-ordered Court. By nature reserved, he was isolated still more by that slight impediment of the speech which made him shun all but formal contacts, except with his familiars. Even his friends he kept at their distance, but with a regular and courteous demeanour that all understood and some, who were formal themselves, grew to like. He was constant in his conduct, predictable, disliking steadily those whom he disliked, holding with great firmness to his opinions and his friends, even when the opinions proved mistaken and the friends faithless, and resolute in the fulfilment of his duty.

He was as fine a judge of horseflesh as he was of painting, and in Sir John Fenwick of Wallington he had a trainer and breeder of high repute, one that "bred the best horses ever was in England for coursing, famous over all the world."[30] In the hunting field the King's formality thawed a little, but never wholly. Deft and lightly made, he rode well; it was necessary that he should. The chase was his passion as it had been his father's, but he was not, like his father, as often in a ditch as in the saddle. "Have I three Kingdoms and must you fly into my eye?" old King James had apostrophised an intruding insect; but the flies, if any, which made this mistake with King Charles were removed without comment. The unseemly, the ludicrous, the merely human were excluded from his public life, and almost all his life was public. Even when he had a hunting accident it was of a high, dramatic kind. Mistaking green weed for a grassy hollow he plunged once in full career into a morass in which his horse irrecoverably floundered. He himself escaped through the prompt assistance of his attendants, and with the utmost coolness, changed clothes with a courtier, mounted a fresh horse and continued the chase.[31]

But though he moved from palace to palace with a restlessness on which foreign ambassadors remarked, he did not know his people well and was a stranger to the greater part of his own dominions. On his journeys he followed always much the same route. He had hunted in the New Forest and visited the Isle of Wight; he went frequently to Newmarket for the races, or to stay with the Earl of Pembroke at Wilton; he had been received at the university of Oxford and he knew the Thames valley and his deer parks at Windsor, Richmond, Oatlands and Theobalds. Once since his manhood, he had travelled to Scotland and back, had seen the wolds of Lincolnshire, had climbed the two hundred and seventy steps of the tower of York Minster to admire the prospect, had crossed the coalfields of Durham, the Northumbrian moors and the hills of Lothian. He had played golf on the links at Leith, and made a progress as far as Perth and Brechin, but, unlike all his ancestors, he had not hunted the deer with the highland clans. He had never been to Wales. He had never visited Ireland. He had inspected his ships of war at Chatham and Gravesend, and had watched, from the sedate summer residence he had built for his Queen at Greenwich, the sails that passed up and down the broad estuary of the Thames to London, but he did not know the seaports of his kingdom or the mariners and merchants on whom the prosperity of his State was so largely built. At his council table, or more informally by conversations in the halls and embrasures of his palaces, he settled a huge number of technical questions relating to taxation, to industry, manufacture and shipping, to the regulation of trade, and the quarrels of his subjects. Through these he had learnt a good many things about the manufacture of salt, soap, pins, and beaver hats, the cloth trade, the importation of wine, the herring fisheries, the oyster beds, the forests, the mines, the foundries and the glass works.

The reports which his Council received regularly from the Justices of the Peace, informed him, if he wished to know, of the general state of the country, the rise or decline of the number of vagabonds, the arrangements for apprenticing orphan children and relieving the industrious poor.

The King had a high sense of duty towards the people whom he regarded as a sacred trust from God, but this was compatible with an open dislike of their proximity and their opinions. It was only, perhaps, when he touched for the King's Evil at Easter and Michaelmas that he allowed the vulgar to approach closely to his royal person, and even then each invalid who presented himself to be cured had to produce a certificate signed by a clergyman, a churchwarden and a justice of the peace before he might enter the palace gates.[32]

He had never had the painful experience from which his father, as a young man, had learnt so much; he had never confronted insolent opponents face to face and had the worst of the argument. No national danger had compelled him to go out among his people and share their perils. He was, at this time, not only the most formal but the most remote and sheltered of all European kings.

Less virtuous monarchs escaped from formality in the arms of low-born mistresses, but for the chaste Charles, no Nell Gwynne, prattling cockney anecdotes, opened a window into the lives of his humbler subjects. What he knew of men, he knew chiefly by report and study. Like many shy, meticulous men, he was fond of aphorisms, and would write in the margins of books, in a delicate, beautiful, deliberate script, such maxims as "Few great talkers are good doers" or "None but cowards are cruel."[33] He trusted more to such distilled and bottled essence of other men's wisdom than to his own experience, which was, in truth, limited; his daily contact with the world was confined within the artificial circle of his Court and the hunting field. He was to say, much later, in tragic circumstances, that he knew as much law as any gentleman in England. It was true; but he had little conception of what the laws meant to those who lived under them.

Admired by some and feared by many, he was not greatly loved. He neither solicited nor gained the affection of his people from whom he expected neither more nor less than duty. In the smaller circle of his Court he was of those who exclude love when they exclude familiarity. His servants knew him to be punctilious and just, a stranger alike to impulses of anger or good humour. In later years the respect which he had from all his household grew into love, but it was his misfortune, not his graciousness, which melted their hearts. In his time of unquestioned power very few felt for him, personally as a man, that unreasonable, human attachment which sweetens service and softens authority.

Yet the King was capable of deep and tender attachment when his secretive affections were touched. His love for his wife, though it had been slow to come, was now the strongest personal emotion in his life.

Queen Henrietta Maria was the opposite of her husband in outward manner and in temperament, and their marriage had opened in storm and rebellion on her side, in a coldness amounting almost to cruelty on his. She was nine years his junior and had come to him as an effervescent girl of fifteen, very fond of dancing. He had objected to her gaieties and to the conduct of the French companions who encouraged her. They had been sent away, leaving the tear-stained child to the mercy of her solemn husband and his overbearing favourite the Duke of Buckingham. For three unhappy years she lived forlorn and neglected; only after the murder of Buckingham, in 1628, did she become pregnant for the first time.

She was not strong and her spine was a little crooked. Her first child, a boy, survived only a few hours and she rose from her bed with the bloom of her youth withered. She had always had bad features, with a long nose and prominent teeth; now the freshness of her complexion and her dimpled charm had gone, though the ivory quality of her skin and her large, brilliant eyes still commanded admiration.

The loss of her looks mattered nothing, for Charles, on Buckingham's death, had transferred his devotion instantly and wholly to his wife. He was in love, with the single-mindedness of those who give their affection to few, but to those few entirely. Beloved, the little Queen flowered again; her vivacity, her charm, and a good dressmaker hid all defects. She knew that she was not a beauty but she made the world think that she was. The dancing, on which the King had frowned, was now permitted, and her wit and gaiety made her husband's Court such as she had always wanted. Year by year her mental ascendancy over her husband increased; he sought her advice on every subject, except religion, and had been heard to regret that he could not make her a member of his council. Only in religion was there no understanding between them, for she was as devoted to the Church of Rome as he to the Church of England.

Sufficient to themselves, the King and Queen were not greatly interested in their growing family. Princes and Princesses were born at regular intervals, at cost of great suffering to the Queen. Suitable attendants were appointed to wait on them and they enjoyed every care proper to their station, but although they accompanied their parents occasionally on a Maying party or courtly revel and Van Dyck painted the Royal Pair awkwardly dandling a couple of babies, neither the King nor the Queen was truly at home in the nursery. Not until years later, when they were themselves separated, did either of them indulge in demonstrations of emotional love for their children.

The Queen had not her husband's studious temperament and slow, ruminative mind. She understood things quickly and superficially; he understood them deeply, or not at all. But like many slow thinkers, he greatly admired a quick wit, and like many doubtful and hesitative men, he was easily impressed by the capacity to make a decision, however ill-conceived or impulsive.

The fusion of their two influences—his for stateliness and form, hers for liveliness and style—had made their Court within a few years the "most sumptuous and happy in the world."[34] The achievement was considerable but it was shallow. It bore no relation to the unsolved problem of government.

II. FAITH AND FOREIGN POLITICS

The King, in agreement with most serious thinkers of his time, believed that good government must be founded on true religion. The first essential was that his people should believe rightly and worship God in the manner most acceptable to Him. What that manner was, the Church alone could teach. Unhappily schism in the Catholic Church and vulgar sectarianism with its hundred disputing tongues made it exceptionally difficult in the seventeenth century to know which belief and which form of worship was right.

The overwhelming majority of the King's subjects, whatever their doctrines, their education or their interests, were simply and sincerely religious. They did not doubt that their souls were immortal or that Christ had died to redeem then. Some of them remembered this daily, most of them remembered it on Sunday, and a few perhaps not more than once or twice a year. But it was to them a cardinal fact in life, and in death. From the felon jauntily going to the gallows, with a bold face and a pious word, to the nobleman (of whom there would soon be many) mounting the steps of the scaffold, almost all faced death with an unquestioning belief in a life to come. The nobleman shared with the felon the uplifting and unshaken conviction that the Son of God Himself had, for his redemption, gone the self-same way. To die without that hope, to die—as men said— "desperately" was an unusual and terrible thing.

The desire to believe and the capacity to believe were still almost equally strong. This was true, with a minority of individual exceptions, of all the King's subjects, in spite of the differences of wealth, breeding and education which divided them.

King Charles counted among his people some of the finest and most cultivated minds in Europe and some of the most primitive. The leading scholars at the universities of Oxford, Cambridge, St. Andrew's, Aberdeen, and the more recently founded Trinity College, Dublin, ranked with the best in the world. Theology dominated the universities but the classics, philosophy, ancient history, mathematics and medicine were also taught. Francis Glisson, lecturing on anatomy at Cambridge, supported William Harvey's new theory of the circulation of the blood, a theory angrily attacked by the Scottish scholar Alexander Ross, who, not content with challenging Harvey and Glisson, was soon to hurl himself with ironical eloquence upon the Italian astronomer Galileo, pulverising him—as he hoped—in a book entitled *The Earth No Wandering Star except in the Wandering Heads of the Galileans*.

London was a centre of scientific activity. At Gresham College, Henry Gellibrand, professor of astronomy, was investigating the magnetic north. The Barber Surgeons company had built an anatomy theatre from designs by Inigo Jones, where public lectures drew distinguished audiences; sometimes banquets were provided, after which the Barber Surgeons, to their chagrin, missed a number of their silver spoons.

Anatomy and all the natural sciences had a great following both amateur and professional. Sir Kenelm Digby was working on an exhaustive inquiry into the *Nature of Bodies* in which he discussed, with other questions, what part of the animal was the first to be formed, whether animals can think and "how the vital spirits are sent from the brain into the intended parts of the body without mistaking their way." Thomas Browne, a physician of considerable reputation who had just settled at Norwich, was compiling an immense and varied store of learning for the book in which he would examine and deal justly with a multitude of common superstitions and vulgar errors in the interests of scientific truth. In Yorkshire, a precocious boy, William Gascoigne, scanned the stars and made improvements in the telescope. It was not three years since the posthumous publication of Dr. Muffet's *Insectorum Theatrum* had opened the way towards the science of entomology.

Mathematicians pursued their solitary calculations. John Napier from his castle tower near Edinburgh had opened the century with the publication of the first tables of logarithms; at another Scottish castle Sir Thomas Urquhart of Cromarty pondered, in his eccentric overcrowded brain, the practice of trigonometry, squaring the circle and the invention of a universal language. William Oughtred had recently published his *Clavis Mathematica*. John Wilkins at Cambridge took time off his mathematical studies to speculate on the habitability of the moon and on an invention, left incomplete, which might have been a telephone. At Cambridge, too, young Seth Ward, poor and studious, wrestled with the problems of geometry. But arithmetic, even in its elementary complexities, was for scholars: in merchants' counting-houses the clerks used the abacus for their sums, although a few now employed an elementary slide rule attributed to John Napier and familiarly known as Napier's Bones. The highly educated and efficient Lord Deputy of Ireland, wishing to reckon fifteen times four, wrote down fifteen four times and added it up. The multiplication table was not at that time taught with the A B C.

The ancient languages of the East and the antiquities of the British Isles exerted a simultaneous attraction upon many scholars. William Bedell, Bishop of Kilmore, the leading Hebrew scholar of the day, had devoted himself since he had gone to Ireland to the study of the Irish language and antiquities and was carefully rendering the Old Testament into Irish. Abraham Wheelocke, Professor of Arabic at Cambridge, who was no less learned in the Persian tongue, after preparing a refutation of the Koran, was translating the works of the Venerable Bede into modern English. Edward Pococke, Professor of Arabic at Oxford, had been granted a sabbatical year to travel dangerously in the Turkish dominions in search of the manuscript treasures of Greek and Syrian monasteries.

The traffic was not all in one direction; Christian refugees from the Turkish dominions sometimes reached England. A Cretan scholar, Nathaniel Canopis, had been brought to Oxford by Archbishop Laud where, from Balliol College, he disseminated his grave learning and amused his colleagues by brewing a black drink from roasted coffee berries.

Scholars in universities and in their homes collected libraries and worked assiduously, together or alone, on problems of history, archæology and etymology never before considered. It was the dawn of the great dictionaries, the surveys, the monumental volumes which laid the foundations of future learning in many different fields. Florio's Italian dictionary, Cotgrave's French dictionary, Minsheu's Spanish dictionary were on the shelves of the learned, as well as Minsheu's remarkable etymological dictionary of nine languages. William Camden's *Britannia* was already a standard work; Dugdale had begun the researches into English ecclesiastical history which culminated in the publication of his *Monasticon*. Henry Spelman had issued the first volume of his glossary of legal terms and was still deeply engrossed midway between M and Z. Dodsworth, Archer, D'Ewes and others were following in the footsteps of Robert Cotton and William Lisle in the study of Anglo-Saxon, revealing the history hidden in place names and the origins of the English language, customs and laws.

The casual tourist had picked up the prevailing intellectual curiosity and would go out of his way to see druidical circles as remote as "Long Meg and her Daughters" in Cumberland. All who crossed the border paused to contemplate the great grass-grown bastion which they vaguely called the Picts Wall. Stonehenge drew travellers to and from the west; Inigo Jones asserted that it had been built by the Romans but other scholars contested this. Visitors to the strange caves of Wookey Hole would play the recorder in order to appreciate the echo.

Lesser, more simply practical or light-hearted speculations and inventions were discussed. Richard Norwood had paced the distance from London to York, a primitive method of measurement which was surprisingly accurate. "Way-wisers" or small machines attached to the leg, or a coach wheel, for measuring the distance travelled, were a discussed novelty. Rival methods of abbreviated writing, the various new stenographies, claimed public attention. John Babington, one of His Majesty's gunners, had borrowed time from his more serious occupations to write a volume on fireworks in which he described "the manner of making the best sort of stars," and "how to make Fisgigs which some call serpents," with such other skilful wonders as coats of arms correctly blazoned or a fortress of fireworks whence mechanical musketeers emerged to fire off rockets— "which being well and orderly performed will give much content."

The London booksellers and printers, congregated about St. Paul's, had an eager market for their wares, paper volumes displayed on trays before their shops, opened at an interesting page. There were books and to spare, good, bad, indifferent, grave, gay, useful, pious. Each was registered at the King's Stationery Office; the harvest of the year 1637 included a commentary on Aristotle by Thomas Hobbes, translations of St. Ambrose, Symmachus, Virgil, Martial and Petrarch; numerous histories ancient and modern; practical handbooks—*The Complete Cannonier or the Gunner's Art, The Attorney's Academy, The Husbandman's Practice, A discourse of Bees;* some works on navigation, on medicine, on midwifery; Taylor's guide to the posts called *The Carriers' Cosmography;* the latest plays of Fletcher, Heywood, and Shirley; *The Merry Jests of the Cobbler of Canterbury* and other familiar joke books; a large number of "dainty new ditties," poems, elegies and anagrams; a new issue of *The Wise Men of Gotham* and other old favourites like the lives of Dick Whittington and Old King Cole; St. Francis de Sales' *Devout Life* in English, a new translation of the Golden *Ass* of Apuleius, and *A Posy of Godly Prayers* from an unknown hand.

In the literary haunts of London—Ben Jonson's old Devil Tavern, or the newer fashioned Rose in Covent Garden, or the Globe, where the walls were painted to represent Arcady—young gentlemen of London and visitors from the provinces talked of the latest books and plays. In country houses, small and great, societies of intelligent men and women met to debate on faith or philosophy, to read their works aloud, to sing or dance together to the pretty music of the virginals or the deeper tones of the small organs which had become popular in many homes. Some have left a name and fame behind, like Great Tew where Falkland's circle met; the pleasures of other great houses are echoed in contemporary letters, Lord Leicester's Penshurst, Lord Northumberland's Syon, Lord Northampton's Compton Wynyates, Lord Newcastle's Bolsover.

Smaller houses, the homes of scholars, clergymen, citizens

and gentlemen, offered the delights of good conversation and sometimes also curiosities and things of beauty to look at. The Provost of Eton, Sir Henry Wotton, collected many friends about him in his peaceful old age to talk of painting and literature, to look at the Venetian pictures that adorned his walls, and to examine such curiosities as "a piece of Crystal Sexangular, grasping divers several things within it, which I bought among the Rhaetian Alps."[1] At the house of his friend Izaak Walton, citizen and ironmonger of London, the talk was of literature and the quiet delights of fishing. Samuel Hartlib, another London citizen, collected about him those interested in education, philosophy or the improvement of husbandry. William Oughtred, in his vicarage at Albury, gathered round him his disciples in the study of mathematics, but would from time to time retire to his room for two or three days together, refusing all food and interruptions, until he had solved the insistent problem tracking through his brain. The poet Drummond, at his secluded Hawthornden in the Lothian hills, discussed poetical and political problems with his kinsmen and friends. Dr. Henry King, in his deanery at Rochester, composed verses and sermons and put together a choice library which he intended to bequeath to the Cathedral.

Such were the pleasures to be found among the most civilised nobility, clergy, gentry and citizens. The average level was not so high. The majority of country houses offered coarse entertainment to the mind: the talk was of dogs, hawks, horses, harvest prospects and local quarrels; the books were manuals on hawking or land tenure, a handbook on the law, the Bible, Foxe's "Book of Martyrs", possibly a play-book bought when last the owner visited London, with *Guy of Warwick, Palmerin of England* or some other romance.

Education of a kind was widespread at least in England. The grammar schools and ancient foundations like Eton, Westminster, Winchester, Charterhouse and St. Paul's, took the sons of citizens and gentry, of the clergy and the professional classes, sometimes those of the nobility. It was more usual for the nobility to have a tutor resident in the house, and for the richer gentry to send the boys to live with a private schoolmaster where five or six pupils, looked after as part of his family, occupied all his scholastic attention. From such establishments, quite as often as from the ancient and famous schools of the realm, the most eminent men emerged.

Hours were long, and six in the morning the usual time for school to begin. Long before daylight on a winter morning schoolboys would be on their way breakfasting, as they went, on a piece of bread and honeycomb or a lump of cheese. At school Latin was the basis of all learning; the boys of the middle and upper classes, when they had mastered the language, proceeded to learn all other subjects, including their own religion, in the Latin tongue. The careful, comprehensive and fundamentally simple catechism which had been prepared in the last century by Dean Nowell for the use of older children was composed in Latin so as to fit into the grammar school curriculum. History, philosophy, geography and all appreciation of poetry or great literature came through the study of ancient and modern Latin classics. History written in English, like Holinshed's Chronicle, or the many recent books on European history were for recreation: so was Raleigh's great *History of the World* —a favourite book among Puritans—which Oliver Cromwell recommended for leisure reading to his idle son Dick.

As Latin was still the universal language of the educated, and modern works both of information and of literature were composed on it, this technique of education did not exclude the boys from contemporary knowledge. On the contrary it brought them into contact with European culture and the greatest of Renaissance and Reformation thinkers. The works of Erasmus, of Melanchthon, of Linacre and of George Buchanan were studied in the grammar schools. Some schools preferred the works of Christian to pagan writers and commended the study of Mantuan, Palingenius or Cornelius Schön, poets and dramatists of the sixteenth century, before those of Lucan, Virgil, Seneca or Terence. The vast corpus of George Buchanan's works, for instance, provided in themselves for English, and still more for Scottish, boys a liberal education;

his writings included plays, epigrams and pastorals, a prose history of Scotland as educational as Livy, and, for political philosophy, his *De Jure Regni* which expounded the theory of a strictly limited monarchy.

The immense influence of Buchanan in the schools had been viewed with disquiet by the late King James, and the Archbishop of Canterbury at this present time was trying to popularise in Scottish schools the fluent verse of Arthur Johnston, recently appointed rector of the university of Aberdeen. Johnston, whose religious views were more favourable to the monarchy than those of Buchanan, had achieved a fair measure of contemporary fame by his recent versification of the psalms in Latin.

The basic Latin of seventeeth-century education did not create uniformity of knowledge or outlook. The majority of Latin-educated boys had no more of the pagan classics than a handful of quotations. Their knowledge, philosophy and outlook on life were drawn from the Latin writers of the last century. But a worldly minority among the nobility and richer gentry had studied the pagan classics, had travelled abroad and had tasted the graces and the civilisation of the antique world in its Renaissance revival. They liked the colour, the imagination, the wit, wisdom and nobility of the Latin poets; they quoted the *Metamorphoses* of Ovid, the Satires of Persius and —more rarely—Juvenal, and above all the stoical and republican sentiments of Lucan's *Pharsalia*. Seneca, beloved of the Elizabethans, was going out of fashion, and Virgil was second to Lucan in favour.

Newer methods were discussed rather than practised. Samuel Hartlib was arranging for the publication in English of the important work on education written by the Bohemian exile John Comenius, and some men of learning hoped that the famous educationist might be persuaded to make his home in the island.

The grammar schools did not undertake to teach the elements of reading and writing. The children of professional men and the gentry were taught their alphabets at home by their mothers, but the ability to read and write was not uncommon among the poor in England, especially in the South. Working women left their children to be minded by some stay-at-home labourer, a cobbler, tailor, weaver, or carpenter. To keep them quiet, he made them learn their letters from a hornbook or battledore with the alphabet pasted upon it, which was handed from pupil to pupil. Dame's schools existed in some villages, but the cobblers' "petty schools" were more usual and some of these amateur schoolmasters, the "abecedarians" as they were called, were patient and clever; one carpenter cut out the letters on blocks of wood, others made up little rhymes, invented small rewards, alternated mental and manual work with play. Girls commonly had less of this schooling than boys; they were not so liable to mischief as their brothers, needed less "minding," and were early able to help their mothers at work. The wilder regions, where farmsteads and hamlets were far apart and no such cobblers' schools existed, were served by travelling pedagogues. These vagabonds of the teaching profession would spend a month or two in one small settlement and then pass on, often following a regular circuit that brought them back once in every three or four years to teach a new gaggle of little children to read and write. The craftsmen who kept school had a halfpenny or a penny a week for each child. The travelling pedagogue was given his keep in one yeoman's kitchen or another, and received presents from grateful parents. It was very simple, primitive and unorganised, but it worked reasonably well. Among the country folk the women were usually illiterate but most intelligent men could read.

They could read: but they had little to read. They read the Bible, for that most decent families possessed. They read Foxe's "Book of Martyrs," the most widespread and popular work of history in England, a copy of which was sometimes kept, along with the Bible, in the parish church. They read elementary books of devotion like *The Practice of Piety* and *The Whole Duty of Man*. Reading little, they took the printed word gravely, pondered it much and remembered it well. The more intelligent thought seriously, because the habit of prayer was usual, and concentrated prayer encourages coherent thinking. In respectable families the parents would possess a cheap catechism and would keep their children thoroughly exercised in it. Furthermore, in all the great schools, in some of the petty schools and in almost every home of whatever kind, everyone sang. The women sang at their carding and knitting and spinning, in the dairy and the kitchen; the men sang at the carpenter's bench, at the loom and the forge, or as they followed the plough. A favourite manual of musical instruction, especially devoted to the singing of the psalms, was reprinted two hundred and thirty-five times in the course of the century.

Where the villages lay thickest, where the market towns were busiest, there the psalms and the Bible-reading, and Foxe's book made their strong impression. For simple people, over the greater part of England and southern Scotland, certain ideas and phrases were written deep on the waxen minds of childhood. An astonished Italian reported that "they give their sons Hebrew names and call their daughters after the virtues and have quite abandoned those in use among Christians."[2] The Old Testament was commonly better known to these people than the New, and unconsciously they acquired the outlook, because they acquired the words, of the Chosen People. To the confident, self-reliant and assertive characteristics of the Anglo-Saxon were added tenacious Jewish fatalism and an unyielding confidence in a God who was theirs against the world.

The danger which might arise from the opinions of people who were serious, literal-minded and only in the most elementary sense *educated* was evident to authority. For this reason the Crown insisted on the importance of catechising children in the hope of keeping the speculations of the humble within the disciplined limits laid down by the Church. From time to time efforts were made to establish some kind of uniformity in the books used for instruction by village pedagogues. In theory, if not always in practice, all A B C's were issued by royal authority, so that nothing but the most orthodox and innocuous prayers or sentences could be found in them. King James had attempted unsuccessfully to coerce all the village dominies in

Scotland into using a text book called *God and the King*, an obsequious treatise by an English divine.

Where the Celtic languages prevailed the scene was different. The adaptable Welsh had partly brought their native culture into line with English fashions. Welsh, alone of the Celtic languages, could claim a reasonable if not a very large number of printed books. A Welsh-Latin dictionary had been compiled and two Welsh aldermen of London had arranged for the printing of a cheap edition of the Bible in Welsh—at five shillings, to suit the slender purses of Welsh farmers. The Common Prayer had been officially translated and a Welsh poet, Edmund Prys, had versified the psalms. Rhys Prichard, an enterprising clergyman, taught his flock in rhyming Welsh, simplifying and even singing the Bible story. But Welsh was no longer the speech of the educated. The Welsh gentry spoke English and sent their sons to English-speaking schools. They did not trouble much with their daughters, and Vicar Prichard, in an angry outburst at the attitude of his compatriots, exaggerated and underlined the different education of Welsh and English girls: an English tinker's daughter could read, he said, when a Welsh squire's daughter could not. Literacy offered little advantage to those who only spoke Welsh, and the poor rarely troubled to learn their letters. Their crafts, their traditions and much of their literature, they handed on by word of mouth.

What was partly true in Wales was wholly true of the Scottish highlands and of Ireland. No useful comparison can be made between the literate Englishman or lowlander and the unlettered Celt. The two did not represent different levels of the same culture; they represented different ways of life and thought. The highlander and the wild Irishman had skills of hand and eye, and a hardiness lost to the southerners; they had knowledge of legend and history and poetry by memory and oral tradition. They had their own code of honour and respected the laws of their ancient, half-shattered society, older than the Norman Conquest, and older than the English invasion. The Anglo-Saxon thought them barbarous, but they thought him vulgar.

The gentry, in the Celtic regions, sometimes sent their sons to English-speaking seats of learning; the highland Scots to Aberdeen and St. Andrews, the Irish to Trinity College, Dublin. But if they were true to the old religion, as many of them were, they sent their sons abroad. Many a young Irish or Scottish chief had his education in France or Flanders, Italy or Spain. They avoided thereby the crude contamination of the Anglo-Saxons but they hardly preserved the purity of their own traditions: Ireland's most distinguished poet of this epoch, Piers Ferriter, a chief dwelling on the Blasket Islands, wrote Petrarchan lyrics in his native tongue.

Romantics and antiquaries regretted that the Reformation and the printed word had had a deadening effect on the natural imagination of the people. John Aubrey lamented that "the many good books and variety of turns of affairs have put all the old Fables out of doors, and the divine art of printing and gunpowder have frighted away Robin Goodfellow and the fairies." His nurse, he said, "had the history from the Conquest down to Carolus I in Ballad." But the English about the year 1637 had not put fables quite out of doors. While some, aspiring to education and picking up undigested knowledge from the new Anglo-Saxon studies, angrily declared that the common people of England were the oppressed descendants of the conquered Saxons while all the nobility were tyrannous Normans, others still accepted the ancient legend that Brutus, a great grandson of Aeneas, had conquered Britain from the giants Gog and Magog. As the power and energy of their country grew, they were well pleased to think that Britain was now what Rome had once been—the legitimate heir of Trojan greatness.

The people were still in many things, and even in their cities, very close to nature and the springs of life. The voices of wind and water, the signs of sun and moon, stars and clouds, the movements of birds, the baying of dogs, had not lost their messages and meanings. Goblins and fairies flittered in the autumn dusk; Robin Goodfellow had "his creambowl duly set" and sometimes, with human connivance, left threepence in the slippers of industrious maids. Pigwiggin afflicted the lazy with cramps; Billyblind chuckled on the hearthstone of the north country cottage; the water nixies clutched at the ankles of the late traveller wading the swollen burn. The wise, wizened faces of the little folk stared at the lone hunter crossing the moors at dusk. At many a cool spring in a shady hollow, sanctified by the name of a maiden saint, loveless girls and barren wives performed rites which had been old when Saint Frideswide was young. Pagan festivals survived, sometimes crudely Christianised; boys and girls decked the houses of town and country with green branches on May Day and danced riotously round the maypole, though the religious, with some justification, abhorred the practice. Crops and wells were blessed with old pagan rites and at harvest festivals straw dolls were plaited and carried in triumph.

In the wilds of Lochaber from time to time a green man would be seen, one that had been killed between daylight and starlight and belonged neither to earth nor heaven. Some thought these apparitions were only the unhappy dead but others thought them one of the many forms taken by the devil. The strong forces of nature, with the advent of Christianity, had become confused with the devil, and after the lapse of centuries witchcraft had become indivisibly compact of pagan and Christian beliefs. The devil, in many forms, bestrode the islands from end to end. Sometimes he was "a proper gentleman with a laced band," as when he came to Elizabeth Clarke at Chelmsford; at other times you might know him, as Rebecca Jones of St. Osyth did, by his great glaring eyes. He was cold and sensual and rather mean: he offered Priscilla Collit of Dunwich only ten shillings for her immortal soul; she gave it to him and off he went without paying. Respectably dressed in "brown clothes and a little black hat," he spoke in friendly terms to Margaret Duchill of Alloa in Scotland; "Maggie, will you be my servant?" he asked, and when she agreed he told her to call him John and gave her five shillings and powers of life and death over her neighbours.[3]

In England the devil kept low company for the most part. He comforted poor, half-crazed, hungry old women, cackling ill-naturedly at their neighbours and growing foolish over a mangy cat, a tame sparrow or a friendly toad on which they

bestowed a comical or high-sounding name, Pyewacket, Jere-
mary, or Grizel Greediguts. In Scotland he was said to have
more distinguished clients. From the spikes on the Tolbooth in
Edinburgh grinned the white skull of the Earl of Gowrie,
reputed a warlock in his time, as other noblemen had been. The
devil drove with Lord Carnegie in a coach-and-six over tracks
where no coach could go. The devil had had a hand in it when
Sir John Colquhoun of Luss seduced his sister-in-law Lady
Katherine Graham, and while the fugitive couple hid in
London, their shocked and distinguished families solemnly
pleaded witchcraft as the cause of their sin. What witch-
crafts flourished among the Celtic peoples is hard to say, but the
English and the lowland Scots viewed their dark powers with
apprehension. The Irish, it was certain, could call up vapours
from their bogs to the destruction of whole armies.

The frontier between legitimate country lore and black
magic was but feebly marked; in general the wise woman or
"cunning man" who collected simples and knew how to brew
drugs or pronounce spells to cure the ills of men and horses, to
take away the toothache, banish warts and ease the pains of
childbed, was not likely to be persecuted as a witch, in England
at any rate. In Scotland, a more austere religious faith made all
rites and jargons suspect, and women who muttered old Latin
rhymes or were guilty of touching a sick cow with a blue pebble
or other such conduct were within reach of the law though it
rarely fell upon them for such things alone.

The "healing touch" was an old English belief. The government sometimes took action against those who claimed to have
it, for to heal by touch was the King's sacred prerogative. A
seventh son of a seventh son—these were popularly thought to
have the power—had practised near London, but his cures were
examined by the College of Physicians and dismissed as fraudu-
lent; he turned out not even to be a seventh son. A little boy
of five in Somerset, who was incontrovertibly a seventh son
of a seventh son, was carried from village to village by his
father and made many cures; no money was paid, only fruit
and sugar-plums, garters, points and ribbons. The Bishop of

Bath and Wells, instructed to look into the matter, was lenient; he let off the father with a caution and sent them both home.[4]

The suppression of superstition and dubious healing rites was but a small part of the King's task. In the matter of witchcraft he had shown himself enlightened, and had intervened to save a group of Lancashire women from malicious persecution. His principal task was the more lofty one of imposing right beliefs and right religious practices on all his subjects, however complex or however simple their minds, however civilised or primitive their way of thought.

To King Charles the Church was the soul of the State, without which the body politic would be inert and lifeless matter. At this tranquil and apparently successful time in his career his feelings for the Church were chiefly apparent in his vigorous determination to destroy its opponents and to enforce upon all his people obedience to its canons. But implicit always in this attitude of his was an inner spiritual passion. His church policy was the outcome not of calculation but of conviction; he was ready to die for it.

In 1637 it seemed impossible that any such sacrifice would be asked of him, yet had the wild hypothetical question been put to him he would not have hesitated in his answer. When he was still a prince, he had been overheard to say to friends that he could not be a lawyer for "I cannot defend a bad nor yield in a good cause."[5]

The sentiment expressed very exactly the King's temperament; when he thought a cause was good he would not yield, and by "not yielding" he did not mean that he would yield on sufficient persuasion, or the day after to-morrow, or the year after next; he meant that he would not yield. This capacity for total resistance showed in these sunnier times as an occasional inconvenient obstinacy: occasional, because the number of things about which the King had completely made up his mind were few. On most subjects his hesitations and indecisions were notorious and embarrassing. But on the question of the Church he was immovable; it was the central pillar of his life, and his attitude to his own royal authority was but a part of his profound conviction of the unique rightness of the Church of England.

He was of the intractable stuff of which martyrs are made—not the swift, ecstatic martyrs who run upon death in a high impulsive fervour, but the sad, thoughtful martyrs who follow over long, patient years some logical sequence of thought and action which always may, and sometimes must, bring them to disaster. It is hard to understand and impossible to do justice to the situation which developed in England unless this peculiar quality of King Charles is seen from the outset as an integral part of it. In 1637 his actions might well be interpreted as those of a King who sought to strengthen the authority of the Crown by extending the authority of the Church. But this was the least part of them; for when it became apparent that their effect was precisely the opposite, that the logic of his policy was leading him not towards a serene magnificence of Kingship but to the mortal hazards of war, to capture, even to death, he would not turn aside.

Charles was the first King who had been brought up from childhood as a member of the Church of England. His predecessors had accepted the Church in maturity, as a convenient framework of belief. Charles had drawn in its doctrine with the innocent acceptance of childhood; the Church of England was to him, as it had been to none of his predecessors, the established order of things.

For the first time, the Anglican Church had as its head a Defender of the Faith who had never considered the possibility of defending any other faith. As if in response to this first monarch, so truly its own, it had flowered into a new beauty, of words, of form, and here and there a shining saintliness. The careful argumentation of Lancelot Andrewes and the menacing thunder of John Donne had been familiar to the King in the early part of his reign, but now a gentler, more pastoral inspiration breathed from the younger generation of preachers, Jeremy Taylor, Henry Hammond, William Cartwright. Many of them wrote poetry; a delicate sensibility to beauty lit up the meditations and prayers which they composed as they contemplated the Infinite from a college study or a vicarage window or the garden of a wealthy patron. They were a minority, as men of sensibility and talent necessarily are, but they set up a vibration in the Anglican community which has not died away. They loved the temperate beauty of their Church, not wantonly glorious like the Church of Rome, nor agressively plain like that of Geneva. As George Herbert gratefully wrote:

> Blessed be God, Whose Love it was
> To double-moat thee with His grace,
> And none but thee.

The King had at his right hand an Archbishop after his own heart. He had always liked and approved of William Laud, although his father had feared the meddling temperament of the little man and had been unwilling to give him preferment. Under King Charles, Laud had been raised first to the see of London, then to that of Canterbury.

A man of great learning, a profound believer in ritual and hierarchy, Laud was more of a tidier-up and setter-in-order than a true reformer, but he had boundless energy and clear, if limited, vision. His ideal was a Church, rigidly and efficiently organised, its services reverently conducted according to a uniform ritual, its hierarchy sagely established, and the whole population gathered together into one docile flock. This vision exactly matched the King's. It became the corner-stone of a deep personal respect and friendship which made it possible for Charles to overlook the Archbishop's social failings. These were less kindly viewed by many of his colleagues on the King's council who found him troublesome, tactless and ill-bred. The son of a Reading tradesman, he had never acquired the poise suitable to his exalted position, and his appearance—"a little, low, red-faced man"— was much against him. He was irritable, opinionated, apt to shout in argument and to slap about impatiently with his hands. He did not have the sense to avoid the absurd; his enemies can be forgiven for their angry amusement when, at the dedication of St. Catherine Cree Church, the splendid opening phrase, "Be ye lift up, ye everlasting doors: and the King of Glory shall come in," was immediately followed by the entry of stout little Laud. In spite of his shortcomings he had an element of greatness, a selfless and singleminded devotion to his religion and his duty. Like the King, he worked not for what he thought to be expedient, but for what he thought to be right, and, like the King, he would not abandon it.

Under the King's and the Archbishop's influence, outward beauty was much regarded. Inigo Jones designed simple, handsome churches in the Renaissance manner, and re-modelled, on chastely luxurious lines, the chapels of the great. Italianate façades and porticoes were wedded incongruously to older buildings. A hybrid style, later to be called Laudian Gothic, was evolved. There was a revived interest in Church plate, vestments, hangings, screens, lecterns, pulpits, fonts, furniture of all kinds, even in painted glass.

Small organs, many of which came from Germany, beautifully carved and gilded, were introduced into private chapels, churches and cathedrals. Singing of the most elaborate kind was encouraged and cherished; new music was composed for the King's chapel and cathedral choirs. The Church flowered in a new beauty of holiness.

George Herbert, a younger son of a noble house, bred to the Court, had abandoned a worldly career and created during his brief devoted ministry the pattern of the Anglican parish priest. Nicholas Ferrar, of a wealthy family, to whom preferment stood open, had withdrawn from the world to Little Gidding in Huntingdonshire, where with his mother and brother and his brother's children he had created a community devoted to prayer, contemplation, good works and religious studies. Poor widows lived on the charity of this community and village children learned their psalms from the pious ladies with a penny prize for the word-perfect and Sunday dinner afterwards for all.[6]

The good preachers, the sensitive writers, the fine, holy and devout men in the Anglican Church were a minority. The King, who drew towards him divines after his own heart, too easily believed that those he saw were, if not typical, at least dominant in the Church. Factious dissent and criticism seemed to him only the last mutterings of an ancient storm soon to be quiet for ever.

He was wrong in every way. His Church was young and insecure, doctrinally divided, imperfectly organised, open to criticism and but feebly rooted in the affections of the people. At the time of its establishment by law under Queen Elizabeth many points of doctrine had been left vague in order that as many as possible of her subjects might be brought in without offence to conscience. The Church was Protestant because it repudiated the Pope but it was officially spoken of as Catholic and it had retained the episcopal hierarchy. This reformation seemed inadequate to the large number of English Protestants who had come under the Calvinist or Baptist influences which flowed into the country with the Netherlands trade. The first demanded the reorganisation of the Church without bishops, on the model of Geneva; the second demanded liberty for congregations of the faithful to choose their own way of worship. Of the two the Calvinist group was the more intellectual, the more highly conscious and the stronger, for the Baptists and their like declined by their very nature towards an anarchy of subdivision.

Apart from those who fully understood the doctrine and organisation of Calvinism, a great number of Protestants in England tended, by temperament, through the verbal interpretation of the Bible or through animosity to the Church of Rome, to lean away from the Catholic and towards the Protestant elements in the Church of England. The term Puritan, used indiscriminately for all these, had no definite and no official meaning: it was a term of abuse merely. It might be applied equally to a devout cobbler expounding the scriptures according to a theory of his own, or to a dutiful member of the Anglican communion who had done no more than hazard the opinion that the surplice was a remnant of Rome.

For the last half-century the English Church had been striving towards a greater clarity and uniformity of worship and doctrine, but the movement had not been continuously in the same direction. Archbishop Whitgift had compelled the more intransigent Calvinist clergy to leave the Church, and his successor Richard Bancroft had worked with pastoral severity to suppress extreme Protestant doctrines. George Abbot, Bancroft's successor, had reversed this policy. He had favoured the more Protestant clergy and discouraged those whose practices showed too close an approximation to Rome.

The doctrines of Arminius, the Dutch theologian who had challenged Calvinism at Leyden, were at this time gaining currency in England and bringing with them a return to ritual. Abbot detested their tenets, but the intellectual fashion was too strong for him; more and more of the promising young men at the universities adopted Arminian views. When King Charles ascended the throne, the division between the Arminians and the school of churchmen whom Abbot approved was already deeply marked. When Abbot retired, Charles himself put forward William Laud, the most distinguished of the Arminians, to take his place. Laud reverted, inevitably, to the anti-Puritan policy of Bancroft and Whitgift. But he could not undo the work of Abbot. The English Church, from bishops downwards, was full of those who disapproved of the Arminians, and Laud's favour towards them was popular neither with laity nor with clergy. "What do the Arminians hold?" went the ill-natured joke—"All the best livings in England." Both pastors and flock were deeply, bitterly divided.

The crucial question was the relationship of the Anglican Church to Rome. The creed spoke of "one holy Catholic Church" but this meant different things to different men. A man who, like the Archbishop or the King, believed that truth was one and indivisible must necessarily wish to see Catholic Christendom reunited. Certain of the Anglican clergy shared the wish, although the intensity of their desire and the ways in which they would have liked to implement it varied greatly. The sincere and unhappily bewildered Godfrey Goodman, Bishop of Gloucester, was one of the few leading churchmen who doubted the rightness of the Anglican position and would have welcomed a return to the communion of Rome at the price of concessions.[7] Archbishop Laud and his chief supporters saw in the Anglican doctrine and ritual the true Catholic faith, deplored the errors of Rome and were steadfast against them. But Rome, for them, represented an error in Catholicism which might one day be set right. It was very different from vile heresies like Calvinism and Baptism. They would protect their flocks with all their strength against conversion to Rome, but they felt the Roman error to be less fundamental and less dangerous to the souls in their care than the sectarian heresies.

The bishops who survived from Archbishop Abbot's time were essentially Protestant and had no thought at all of undoing the work of the Reformation. Several of them were distinguished for discretion and integrity but they were not fortunate in their leadership. Bishops Davenant of Salisbury and Hall of Exeter, learned and worthy men, were neither of them ambitious for domination. The able and diplomatic Bishop Morton of Durham was equally unwilling to thrust himself forward in Church politics. Leadership of the group who wished to conciliate the Puritans fell therefore to John Williams, Bishop of Lincoln, a super-subtle Welshman against whom the Archbishop waged a continual war. Williams believed, honestly and charitably, that the Church could prosper only through alliance and friendship with the best of the Puritans. But his honesty of motive did not go with honesty of method. Mistakenly meddling in the early quarrels of Charles and his Parliaments, Williams had forfeited the King's favour and laid himself open to the grave charge of revealing state secrets. In attempting to defend himself against this charge, the excitable and over-ingenious prelate had involved himself in an offence even more grave—that of suborning witnesses. The King, dropping the original accusation, had substituted the new one, and Williams, after trying every trick of evasion and postponement, was to face the King's council in the summer of 1637 on this disgraceful charge. So shocking a crime made him at the moment more of a liability than an asset to the conciliatory party in the Church. The Archbishop, well knowing this, pressed the charge home with the intention of wrecking, at one blow, both Williams and the policy for which he stood.

The division between the best men in the Church was one grave difficulty that the King had to face. Another problem was the inadequate resources and organisation of the Anglican Establishment. At the untidy Reformation made by Henry VIII the economic foundations of the Church had been irreparably damaged. The hierarchy and the administrative framework had survived and been reaffirmed under Elizabeth, but it was another matter to restore enough Church property to maintain the Anglican Church with the dignity of its Roman predecessor. The bishoprics had been so plundered that Elizabethan, Jacobean and Caroline bishops were reduced to the oddest expedients. The Bishop of St. David's tore off and sold all the lead on the episcopal palace. The Bishop of Lichfield recklessly deforested his land to get the profit of the timber. Other bishops converted the short leases of their tenants into life-rents for sums of ready money. This was a help to the bishop who made the arrangement but left his successor poorer than before, and King Charles had vigorously—and vainly—prohibited the practice.[8]

Since the Reformation, tithes had in some places been commuted for money, and in others been alienated to the lay patrons of the living. The value of money had declined in the past eighty years and often changes in agriculture had altered the value and quantity of the payments in kind. Friction over tithes between the clergy and their parishioners or their patrons was frequent, and was intensified by the contention of Puritan dissidents that they did not wish to pay any minister who was not of their own way of thinking, or even that to pay tithes at all was a form of simony, the gifts of the Holy Ghost not being for sale. All these quarrels brought to popular notice the least spiritual aspect of the Church and its ministers.

Patronage of church livings had at the Reformation been greedily swallowed up by laymen of all sorts, landowners or corporations, who had frequently taken a large part of the endowments as well. The smallness of the incomes from preferments led to unashamed pluralism. A churchman who by astute courting of the right patrons had procured several livings for himself could delegate his religious duties to one or two poor curates hired at miserable wages. The pluralist himself, it was said, "weareth cassocks of damask and plush, good beavers and silk stockings, can play well at tables or gleek, can hunt well and bowl very skilfully ... and can relish a glass of right claret."[9] The absentee was rarely an advertisement for the

spiritual qualities of the Church, nor was the starveling curate
who filled his place.

The parson's status in the social hierarchy was doubtful;
manual labour was frowned on but he had to work his glebe.
Parishioners in one village complained because the parson
played ninepins with the butcher, and in another, because he
undertook odd jobs of thatching in his spare time. No doubt
much depended on the reputation and general behaviour of
individuals: many of these disappointed educated men, exiled
in remote places, found solace in drink and low company, and
thatching or playing ninepins with the butcher were only one
part of the conduct which was felt to misbecome their office—
for when the neatly dressed parson's wife of Fladbury tripped
down the village street with her milk pail on her head like a
dairymaid she got nothing but indulgent smiles and commenda-
tions for her Christian simplicity.[10]

Ordination was inadequately controlled. Orders were sold
or forged, or given by bishops on insufficient inquiry into the
character and education of the candidate. The Puritan Baxter's
account of the Anglican clergy round Kidderminster at about
this time—decrepit and doddering or else drunk and immoral—
represents the Church as seen by a vehement critic, but these
dark colours were true to a part of the reality. The Church had
neither the men nor the organisation to meet all the needs of the
people. Wales was wretchedly neglected for lack of priests and
of those appointed to Welsh parishes few could speak or preach
in Welsh. In Herefordshire it was said that in over two hundred
churches and chapels there were not twenty incumbents fit or
willing regularly to preach a sermon.[11]

Serious-minded men and women, some but not all of whom
were extreme Protestants, tried to remedy the shortcomings or
the absence of the local clergy by meeting independently for
prayer and Bible reading. It was an easy step from this to expounding and preaching. A gentleman living in Exeter, for
instance, with a comfortable household employing seven or
eight servants, held "a conference upon a question propounded
once a week in his own family"—a debate upon the scriptures

in which his children and servants joined.[12] However innocently such discussions began, they created a dangerous liberty of argument, and the established Church discouraged them, mildly or vigorously according to the temper of the bishop in charge. Attacks provoked defiance and bred fanaticism; in districts where Puritanism was deeply rooted, family gatherings insensibly grew into conventicles, meeting secretly when they were forbidden. The steady increase in the number of these conventicles was, for all those who had the interests of the Establishment at heart, one of the most disquieting phenomena of the sixteen-thirties.

A group of Puritans, earlier in King Charles's reign, had embarked on a scheme for providing respectable clergy by private enterprise. They bought in advowsons which had become secularised at the Reformation, and presented to them ministers of their own choosing. In this way they planned, little by little, to place men of good morals and sound doctrine—according to their way of thinking—in a great number of parishes. They had not gone far before they were stopped. In Laud's opinion their action was a plot—"in a cunning way, under a glorious pretence, to overthrow the Church government, by getting into their power more dependency of the clergy, than the King and all the Peers and all the Bishops in all the Kingdom had."[13]

From his own point of view Laud was right, but so, from their point of view, were the Puritan gentry who had given time, thought and money to the project. Both wanted to propagate what they took to be right doctrine and both wanted control of the best instrument of instruction and propaganda in the country—the pulpit.

Whitgift and Bancroft in their efforts to reorganise the Church had made great use of one effective weapon, the ecclesiastical Court of High Commission for inquiring into abuses. Under Bancroft clashes with the common lawyers began to arise; the High Commission, as the guardian of public morals, claimed jurisdiction in numerous domestic disputes and also in cases arising on, or in connection with, church land. Disputes over tithes also brought the interests of the Church into contact and collision with the common law[14] and the possibilities of ecclesiastical encroachment on territory belonging to the secular courts yearly increased; the old medieval conflict between spiritual and secular justice was thus revived. The danger to the Church arising from this clash with the common law was immediate and practical, for the pretensions of the High Commission Court created an alliance between the common lawyers and the Puritans.

Archbishop Laud used the High Commission vigorously, both to enforce his doctrinal and ritualistic ideas and to maintain the purity of English morals. Those summoned before the Court were compelled to take the so-called *ex officio* oath before answering the searching questions which might be put to them. Refusal to take the oath or to answer any question was treated as a plea of guilty. This practice above all roused the anger of the lawyers and caused popular critics to compare the High Commission, with sincere exaggeration, to the Spanish Inquisition.

Meanwhile, cases for quarrel with the extreme Protestants both clergy and laity, increased from year to year. Candles multiplied in the churches of the young, fervent Arminian clergy whom Laud favoured; images of saints and of the Virgin were restored or introduced; the Communion table was set up altarwise at the east end of the chancel. The Arminian clergy wore not only the surplice but vestments; a silly woman in Norwich, seeing something red, asked why the Mayor was officiating in church. Music came back to the cathedrals; choir boys were taught to come in two by two and not to turn their backs to the altar; priests bowed towards it; some even used the sign of the Cross.

The more extreme opponents clamoured derisively about these "apish anticks," these cringings and duckings and caperings, and a great number of simple people were truly perturbed and bewildered at what they believed to be a return to Rome. Knowing their Bible and Foxe's "Book of Martyrs," and remembering, in grisly detail, how some of their immediate forefathers had endured martyrdom rather than yield to the idolatries of Rome, they were profoundly unwilling to betray the faith which had thus been sealed and sanctified to them. It was useless to explain to such people that an image is not in itself idolatrous but only becomes so when it is worshipped as an idol; this seemed to them mere sophistry against the forthright words of the second commandment: *Thou shalt not make unto thee any graven image.*

So also with the commandment to keep holy the sabbath day, a commandment notoriously flouted by the Papists. In some regions of the country, where the old religion was still strong, the sabbath-keepers and the sabbath-breakers came into open conflict. In Lancashire and in Somerset wakes and holy days were enthusiastically celebrated by some, in defiance of the pious disapproval of others. King James had attempted to make an end of the people's quarrels by issuing a judgment of Solomon in the matter. In 1618 he had published the *Book of Sports* declaring what games might lawfully be played on Sundays after church: he included dancing for both sexes, vaulting, archery, and maypoles and morris dances in season. The King had prefaced his Book with the argument that if sports were made unlawful, the people would be driven to tipple in alehouses where they would learn to indulge themselves in "idle and discontented speeches."

The Book was, in intention, both politic and humane but it met with great opposition. King Charles reissued it in 1633 with instructions that the vicar of each parish see that its provisions be thoroughly made known. He was widely reported to have commanded the clergy to read it from the pulpit, and some do indeed seem to have understood his orders in this way, for one, who read the book, followed it with the fourth commandment, adding, "Dearly beloved, you have heard the commandment of God and Man: obey which you please."

The Archbishop's more indiscreet supporters often aroused the animosity of their flock. A vicar of Grantham provoked derision because he genuflected with such extravagance as to lose his balance. A little later, when he tried to move the communion table to the east end of the chancel, his parishioners burst into the church to stop him. The vicar tugged at one end, they at the other, till he gave up the unequal contest, shouting to them to keep their old trestle, he would build a stone altar instead. They would have no "dressers of stone" in their church, they retorted and, led by a couple of aldermen of their city, went off in a party to complain to the Bishop. The vicar followed after, "pale and staring in his looks," pitifully telling the Bishop that his parishioners had threatened to burn his house.

The diocese was Lincoln and the Bishop John Williams, the conciliator. He asked them all to supper and tried to patch up the quarrel. Later he wrote to the vicar: "Whether side soever, you or your parish, shall yield unto the other, in these needless controversies, shall remain in my poor judgment, the more discreet, grave and learned of the two: and by that time you have gained some more experience in the cure of souls, you shall find no such ceremony equal to Christian charity."[15] Not long after he published, anonymously, in a pamphlet entitled *Holy Table: Name and Thing* his own moderate opinion on the place of the communion table in churches. The Archbishop regarded this attempt to propound a calmer view of the controversy with nothing but resentment.

Other church dignitaries were intransigent with their flocks for more secular reasons. At Chester no mayor had entered the cathedral for twelve years, owing to a dispute about the place allotted to him. At last a mayor, who had begun life as a cathedral chorister, tried to heal the breach but no sooner did he attempt to take his seat in the cathedral than the Dean reopened the old dispute and the mayor did not come again.[16]

Sometimes the internal dispute in the Church flared up between members of a cathedral chapter. A prebend of Durham, John Cosin, persuaded the chapter to beautify this most splendid of cathedrals in a worthy manner: great candlesticks gleamed on a high altar of "branched marble" and old defaced carvings of saints and angels were restored. A rival Puritan member of the cathedral chapter, Dr. Smart, in a thundering sermon on idolatry condemned him as "our young Apollo, who repaireth the Choir and sets it out gaily with

strange Babylonish ornaments.'' The Court of High Commission silenced Smart, who lost his place in the cathedral and
was fined five hundred pounds. The sentence purchased a
temporary victory for Cosin at far too high a price; in the angry
Puritan world Smart became the proto-martyr in a new era of
persecution.[17]

Whatever the occasional extravagances of the Laudians, the
conduct of the English in Church at this epoch stood in need
of reformation. Lack of money and the disappearance of endowments had caused many churches to fall into decay and
some altogether into disuse. Many were filthy, with unglazed
windows, and mud floors like cow byres. Squatters took possession of neglected chapels; in Wiltshire several families were
found camping in one, using suitable tombstones as cheese
presses.[18] The abhorrence of idolatry taught by the Puritans had
degenerated into open disrespect for church buildings. The
parish church was often the parish meeting place, not only for
sober business but for dancing and drinking parties. Sporting
parishioners brought their dogs and hawks to divine service
and the poorer sort pastured their hogs in the graveyard. An
indignant sexton in Suffolk found the local squire sheltering
from a storm with his horse inside the sacred building.

Much Communion plate had vanished at the Reformation
and its place was often meanly supplied by wicker and earthenware bottles and vulgar tavern pots. The Calvinist practice of
giving the sacrament at a table placed in the middle of the nave
was usual; this, in Laud's angry phrase, made the church into
an alehouse. He exaggerated, but the central position of the
Communion table encouraged the congregation to use it as the
common repository for hats and gloves, and to loll upon it with
their elbows during the sermon.[19]

Social distinctions were more carefully preserved than rever-
ence towards God. The gentry, and the London apprentices,
thought it beneath their dignity to sit bareheaded during the
sermon. In Bristol it was customary to wait for the mayor before beginning the sermon, or, if he came early, to begin the
sermon immediately, omitting all the rest of the service. The
clergy in many towns seem to have thought it right or at least

advisable to "give good-morrow to Mr. Mayor, though in the middle of the Lesson." Conversely a respectful ploughman, joining in the responses, was alleged to have answered the vicar's *The Lord be with you* by *And with your worship's spirit.*

Such was the situation which the King and the Archbishop undertook to reform. Not long after the unseemly tumult between the vicar of Grantham and his parishioners, Laud began to insist that the communion table in every church in the kingdom be moved to the east end of the chancel and protected by rails "one yard in height and so thick with pillars that dogs may not get in."[20] The wearing of the surplice, bowing at the name of Jesus, and the churching of women after child-birth (another ceremony repugnant to the extreme Protestants) were likewise to be enforced.

Year after year, by means of visitations and prosecutions in the ecclesiastical Court, the Archbishop pressed on with his counter-reformation, provoking at each new clash and at each new prosecution a deeper resentment against himself and against his King.

The intensity with which his orders were enforced varied from diocese to diocese. In the south and south-west, the old and cautious Bishop Davenant of Salisbury and the gentle and humane Bishop Hall of Exeter were anxious not to drive good men into opposition for trifles or to provoke animosity among the people. Neither of these bishops was popular at Whitehall, and Charles had had each of them in turn—and Hall more than once—on his knees before the Privy Council for offending his religious susceptibilities. The Dean of Winchester, also, pleaded to be excused from bowing at the name of Jesus because of the offence which this gave to the ignorant and to weaker vessels who might be alienated and lost to the Church.[21]

Very different was the spirit of the vehement Arminian, Matthew Wren, who had been appointed to the see of Norwich in the heart of East Anglia, the stronghold of Puritanism. The vigour of his visitations and the searching character of the questions which were put to the people had, within the space of two years, created a sullen, vindictive resentment throughout his diocese. He inquired not merely into the state of churches and churchyards, the order of services, the dress of the clergy, the existence of conventicles, the employment of chaplains or tutors by private families, but asked whether any man had heard any other speak anything against the King's authority, or if any in the parish did "presume to make matters of divinity their ordinary table-talk." If there were any who took "the liberty of their trencher-meetings ... rashly and profanely to discourse of Holy Scripture" it was the duty of their neighbours to "name the persons, times and places, as far as you know, or have heard or can remember."[22] This gave dangerous encouragement to informers, provoked suspicion and ill-feeling from many honest, earnest Christians, and instituted a prying, exacting inquiry which was deeply resented. The number of prosecutions in the diocese and the number of the clergy suspended for Puritan conduct or doctrine was, in truth, nothing out of the ordinary. But the anger aroused by the bishop's policy was not assuaged because he was less terrible in deed than in word.

A recently published pamphlet called *News from Ipswich* had given the Puritans of London an exaggerated account of the troubles in East Anglia. Written in a confused but passionate manner, full of rhetoric, but also full of lively details, the pamphlet was widely bought and read before the government could stop it. The source of the publication was never revealed. It bore the statement "printed in Ipswich," but no Ipswich printer had set it up. A popular London preacher, Dr. Henry Burton, the Puritan rector of St. Matthew's, Friday Street, made *News from Ipswich* the subject of two sermons, in which he loudly condemned not only Bishop Wren but all bishops as "upstart mushrumps." This was not the first time that Burton had offended and he cannot have been greatly surprised at finding himself once again the object of government prosecution. In June of the year 1637 he faced his trial before the King's council, with two other opponents of the bishops.

The authorship of *News from Ipswich* had been traced to William Prynne, once a barrister, now a prisoner in the Tower of London. Some years before he had been condemned for the publication of a violent attack on the stage, a work as erudite as

it was intemperate, entitled *Histriomastix*. The book was alleged to contain references to the dancing and masquing at
Court and thus to offend the King's—and more especially the
Queen's—Majesty. Prynne had been fined £5,000, had stood
in the pillory, had had his ears cut off, and been sent to the
Tower for life. Oxford had taken away his degree, Lincoln's
Inn had expelled him, and the Inns of Court, to show their
abhorrence of his opinions, had presented Shirley's famous and
fabulously expensive masque, *The Triumph of Peace,* as a
special compliment to the Court.

Prynne's powerful intellect and massive learning were con-
stricted within the rigid bonds of his fanatical prejudices. He
had no interests outside the study, no wife, few friends, and he
advocated his Calvinist convictions with the glum ferocity of
the professional pedant. He was an exasperating, unloved, un-
lovable man but his single-minded and ill-placed courage were
to make him, over the years, into a popular public character.

Side by side with Henry Burton and William Prynne stood
John Bastwicke, one of Burton's parishioners. By profession a
doctor, Bastwicke had also been in trouble before and had been
imprisoned in the Gatehouse for publishing in the Latin tongue
attacks on the bishops. Early in 1637 he had changed his
manner, though not his matter, and published an attack in
plain English. All three men were thus before the Council for
the same offence: a deliberate attempt to undermine the hierarchy of the Church. Prynne, Burton and Bastwicke might each
individually be dismissed as a cantankerous eccentric. But they
voiced an opposition which was steadily growing.

The opposition was serious, although often expressed in an
ignorant, factious and ridiculous manner. Henry and Susan
Taylor, from a Norfolk village, had, for instance, loudly babbled
that bishops were lazy fellows, that tithes were unlawful, that
the Anglican service was no different from the Mass and—with
an unexpected veering from Protestantism to Popery—that the
clergy should not marry.[23] The vicar of Llanidloes, who let his
parishioners shoot birds in the nave and cut up his surplice for
towels, was of much the same mettle as the Essex woman who
pegged up her laundry in the chancel, crying that if parson

brought his old linen into the church, so would she; or the good
wife in Wolverhampton who, on being told to wear a veil for
her churching, impudently clapped a dinner napkin over her
head. Now and again the extremist fringe showed signs of
mental derangement; the crazy Lady Eleanor Davies, who had
the reputation of a prophetess, marched into Lichfield cathedral
with a bucketful of pitch and splashed it over the altar hangings;
she was assisted by the town clerk and his wife, both of
whom seem to have been sane.[24] All this was ridiculous; but
the popular emotions and the deeper convictions which under-
lay these incidents were not ridiculous.

The King's attitude to sermons stirred the Puritans more
deeply than his attitude to ceremonies. The sermon, the expounding of the scriptures, was their great strength; when a
parson was himself weak in this kind of eloquence it was not
unusual for him to engage, often at the expense of the parish,
a lecturer to do the preaching for him. The great majority of
these were Puritan clergy who, in present circumstances, were
unlikely to get any higher preferment. Where Puritanism was
strong, parishioners sometimes joined together for the godly
purpose of paying for extra sermons, usually mid-week lectures.
In this way, without any direct contravention of the authority
of the Church, extreme Protestantism was poured forth from
a great number of pulpits.

The King and the Archbishop, determined to stop the abuse,
decreed that one sermon on Sunday, on a strictly uncontroversial
topic, was alone to be permitted. Suitable sermons for general
use were available, to help the less eloquent, in the *Book of
Homilies*. At afternoon service a general catechism was to take
the place of the sermon. As for the mid-week sermons, they
were only to be allowed under strict diocesan supervision. Two
more Puritan devices were forbidden: the church bell was not
to be rung in a special manner to distinguish a service with a
sermon from one without, and popular preachers were no
longer to hold their services either later or earlier than those of
neighbouring clergy, to enable people from outlying parishes to
combine them, on a Sunday, with compulsory worship in their

own church. In future there was to be no question of sermon-hungry parishioners straying into other folds to taste forbidden fruit.[25]

Apart from this general prohibition, the Archbishop and the bishops who supported his policy, from time to time suspended individual clergy or prohibited them from preaching. In Wales, the ignorance of the people and the isolation of farms and hamlets caused a few conscientious clergy to preach out of doors, in farm houses, or at irregular hours. William Wroth of Llanfaches, accused of such practices before the High Commission, pleaded with Celtic passion. He had seen "thousands of immortal souls around me, thronging to perdition, and should I not use all means to save them?" He was deprived of his cure none the less; so was William Erbury, of St. Mary's Cardiff and his curate, Walter Craddock. These three devout evangelists were strongly marked with Puritanism and, on losing their cures, continued to preach privately in despite of the law; Craddock ("a bold ignorant young fellow," said the High Commission) took his staff and scrip and roamed the hills of South Wales expounding the word of the Lord to the people in their own tongue. But even the gentle Rhys Prichard, who was no Puritan, was in trouble with authority for his unconventional practice of teaching the scriptures by making and singing Welsh songs with his flock. The Archbishop, whose first bishopric had been the South Welsh diocese of St. David's, was willing enough that the light of the gospel should shine in Wales, but it must shine only as he directed.

Clergy who had clashed with the Archbishop did not easily escape his vigilance. Thomas Shepard, a young man who shortly after his ordination had been chosen as their lecturer by the people of Earl's Colne in Essex, was one of those forbidden either to preach or to exercise any other religious function. He vainly argued his case in an interview with Laud, but the Archbishop trembled with rage and looked, Shepard recorded, "as though blood would have gushed out of his face." Shepard and his friends, who were no more courteous to Laud than he to them, spoke of him among themselves as the swine sent "to root up God's plants in Essex." Uprooted, Shepard fled to Yorkshire where he took refuge in a private household, but his retreat was discovered and he sailed for the wider freedom of New England.

New England and the other settlements far across the Atlantic were a source of nagging annoyance to the Archbishop and the King. It was difficult to know for sure, and almost impossible to stop, what was going on in those places. The Archbishop did his best by persistently interfering with the efforts of Puritans to raise money for "godly ministers" to go out to the congregations across the Atlantic. The stream of emigration of Puritan congregations and their clergy went on none the less and the King was now seriously considering a total prohibition of all further sailings.

An annoyance of another kind came from the Protestant shores of Europe. English clergymen ordained by Calvinists in Holland somehow made their way into the English Church, and several protests to the Prince of Orange not to permit this irregular ordination of Englishmen had hitherto been in vain. Enclaves of foreign Calvinism also remained within the King's dominions. The Channel Islanders had received the Reformation from France and were indifferent to the English-speaking version of it later dispensed to them. Allowances had to be made for the Channel Islanders; they enjoyed a good many separate rights, owing to their status as part of the lost Duchy of Normandy. Administrative quarrels, bitter and frequent at this time, were not Laud's province: religion was. He went to work with more restraint and wisdom than usual. The difficulty was that all instruction in the islands had to be in French, and teachers were usually trained at the Huguenot academy at Saumur. Laud endowed three fellowships for Channel Islanders at Oxford in the hope that good education and pure doctrine would flow forth together from his own university.

The refugee churches, founded by fugitives from the Spanish Netherlands or France, and scattered over the south and south-east—at Norwich, Colchester, Maidstone, Sandwich, Canterbury, Southampton and London—came in for rougher treatment. Wren attacked them in the Eastern counties, Laud in the diocese of Canterbury. Their reason for existence as communities was questioned and they were commanded to attend the English parish churches and dissolve their separate organisation. Their English fellow citizens took their side; quite apart from the religious aspect of the matter, the towns which sheltered them did not want their own parishes to become responsible for the poor and infirm of communities which had hitherto always looked after their own.[26]

The English Church covered England and Wales and enclosed at least two-thirds of the King's subjects, willingly or unwillingly, within the fold. The Churches of Ireland and Scotland, which also engaged the King's attention, offered different problems. The Church of Ireland was, in organisation, doctrine and liturgy, the same as that of England, and the King usually sought the advice of Laud in making appointments to Irish bishoprics, in spite of the primacy, over the Irish Church, of James Ussher, Archbishop of Armagh.

Ussher's Anglican flock consisted chiefly of settlers and their families. Ineradicable and all-pervasive, the Old Religion commanded the allegiance of the Irish; the Roman priests and bishops had their loyalty although cathedrals, churches, chapels, and episcopal residences and revenues were in the hands of strangers, and their own clergy lived on the charity of the faithful by the sufferance of the government.

Abroad, in Rome, in Spain, in the Spanish Netherlands, Irish friars kept in constant touch with their brethren at home. Plots for the return of Ireland to the Church, with the help of Spain, were continuously in the air. A mysterious figure, the titular Archbishop of Cashel, moved secretly between Ireland and Spain; it was said that the Spaniards paid him a thousand ducats a year for his services, and the Lord Deputy Wentworth had hitherto been unsuccessful in identifying and seizing upon him.[27]

The Church of Ireland was adrift like a raft on an alien sea, and had not even the universal approval of the settlers who were inclined, especially in Ulster, towards the anti-episcopal doctrines of Calvin. It was at least fortunate in the Primate, James Ussher, Archbishop of Armagh. He was "a tall, proper, comely man," of a fine but austere presence, studious and frugal habits and simple, courteous bearing. Ussher's Protestantism was enriched by great learning, guided by a high intelligence and informed by a genuine, though concealed, warmth of heart. He was a man of strong, unbending character but he was not provocative. Laud, who did not agree with him, respected both his knowledge of Ireland and his integrity; he never willingly went against him either in his appointments or his policy, and the Irish Church had been allowed to retain an essentially Protestant character. The English Church in Ireland had, however, suffered no less than the Church at home from the unscrupulous plundering of its revenues since the Reformation. The ceaseless law suits about property and endowments between the clergy and the laity made it unpopular with the wealthy settlers and sometimes contemptible to the pious.[28]

In Ulster the Lowland Scots who had come over in the last twenty-five years were emphatically Calvinist, often gave trouble to their bishops and were sometimes abetted in it by their own clergy. Since defiance of authority could not in any circumstances be tolerated, Archbishop Ussher, though not altogether happy about the matter, was at one with the Lord Deputy Wentworth in disciplining the recalcitrant. A number of the more stubborn had been deprived of their livings and made to leave the country. The Bishops of Down and Derry were the firmest in carrying out this policy, a circumstance which (because of the refrain of the old song—*hey derry down derry*) provoked a grim smile even among the Puritans.

Some of these expelled Scottish clergy had set sail for New England, but contrary winds had driven them back to the Ayrshire coast, where they were joined by others who had had to leave Ireland. Their forlorn condition touched the good people of these parts, especially the women, and the strong-minded housewives of Ayr came to Edinburgh to plead their cause. When the King's councillors tried to pass them by, their spokeswoman laid a muscular hand on the arm of the foremost with "Stand, my lord, in Christ's name, till I speak to you."[29]

Most of the King's councillors in Scotland were anxious to yield to Calvinist opinion whenever possible, for the religious situation, complicated by economic anxieties and national pride, was more immediately dangerous there than in either of his other kingdoms. Seventy years before, Scotland had been the scene of a violent Calvinist Reformation. The bitterness of feeling between Calvinist and Catholic had been further intensified by the racial antagonism of Saxon and Celt; the old religion survived in the restless highlands but the industrious people of the lowlands turned to the new.

King James VI had sidled his way through the savage factions of his nobility until he achieved effective authority over the warring elements in the Scottish state. Catholicism survived illegally in the wilds, but he made the nation's official religion Protestant, while steadily discouraging its more extreme manifestations. By the exercise of patience and ingenuity and the offer or distribution of bribes, King James had persuaded succeeding Assemblies of the Kirk to accept the return of episcopacy and to pass orders for church worship and organisation—the famous Five Articles of Perth—by which kneeling to receive the sacrament, confirmation by bishops and the principal fasts and feasts of the Church were restored. Further he had not tried to go, and he had been constant always to one important principle of policy: to do nothing likely to unite the interests of the nobility with those of the extreme Calvinists. He had been careful, when restoring the bishops, to make no attempt to restore also the episcopal revenues seized by lay landowners at the Reformation. The Jacobean bishops were humble and cautious men careful to placate the secular lords. King James had, moreover, left the parish organisation of the Kirk intact, so that the system of moral and religious control in each village and community was on the Geneva model, with elders and frequent meetings to maintain discipline and to control alike the minister and the people.

King Charles was unwilling to acquiesce in this middle part. When he visited Scotland—which was not until the ninth year of his reign—he introduced the full Laudian ceremony at the chapel of Holyrood. The coronation was marked by a clash of wills with the Lord Chancellor, who threatened to resign rather than give precedence, at the King's request, to the Archbishop of St. Andrews. "I will not meddle further with that old cankered goutish man," said the King angrily as he yielded the point. In outward form the coronation was, otherwise, according to the King's desire, but the hearts of his nobility did not go with their hands. Lord Rothes, who carried the Sword at the ceremony, attempted some days later to present a petition against the bishops.[30]

Parliament, meeting during the King's visit, passed some further reforms in ceremonial with only a narrow majority—some said with no majority at all, but by the juggling of the clerk who was a King's man. Charles noted the names of all who had voted against the measure and when, not long after, one of them, Lord Balmerino, was found to be in possession of a draft of another petition against prelacy, the King had him arrested on a charge of high treason. Tried by the King's council and condemned by a casting vote, Balmerino was then graciously reprieved by the King. He felt no gratitude, only a smouldering resentment at a monstrous proceeding.

The passions raised by the Balmerino trial and the unwillingness of so many of his peers and people to accept further changes in ceremony and ritual should have opened the King's eyes to the difficulties which lay before him in trying to make the Scottish Church as like the English as possible. But the King was in no position to make dispassionate judgment. The courtier-Scots whom he kept about him in England were willing and obedient Anglicans; those who had been most forward and most favoured in Scotland during his visit had also been, either from conviction or from policy, episcopalian in sympathy. Drummond, the poet-scholar, who had composed the official welcome to the King, was a convinced episcopalian; so were several distinguished scholars and clerics, especially those from the university of Aberdeen. The distinction and eminence of these Scottish episcopalians concealed from the King the relative smallness of their numbers. A Court religion will always be in some degree a fashionable religion, and in Edinburgh in the thirties persons of rank frequently attended the Anglican service at the Chapel Royal. The Anglican service was also used by one or two of the younger bishops in their chapels and at New

College, St. Andrews—all this with no noticeable protest, or none that reached the King's ears. He came to believe, on evidence all too slight, that the old stubbornness of the Calvinist Scots had weakened, and continued firmness would break it down altogether.

More truly religious and less wary than his father, Charles had from the outset abandoned political caution when faith and the honour due to the Church were in question. His attempt to make the Chancellor give way to the Archbishop, and his regular appointment of bishops to the vacant places on his council in Scotland, was deeply disturbing to the Scots. When in 1635 the Chancellor died, the Archbishop of St. Andrews was appointed to his place. The nobility, who were willing enough to tolerate bishops as inferiors, were indignant at this new elevation. They saw in it an attempt of the King to govern Scotland by means of his own prelatical nominees. The situation was not improved by the character of some of these. The Archbishop was old and careful to placate when he could. But the younger generation of bishops were bolder men, more zealous for the King's policy; they were prepared to outface the nobility and to respond to rudeness, not with Christian resignation but with episcopal dignity. Personal quarrels occurred even at the council table. So far from strengthening his council in Scotland by appointing bishops to it, the King weakened it by multiplying causes for hostility and division among its members.

The Scots nobility, on and off the Council, had another reason for resenting the King's religious policy. He had already proclaimed his intention of restoring to the Church some, if not all, of the property which they had seized. His two principal Scots courtiers, Lennox and Hamilton, had agreed to sell back to the Crown, for the Church, lands that their fathers had taken. The good example was not followed by other lords, who felt a growing apprehension for the safety of their property.

The King had not revisited Scotland, but in the four years since his coronation he had continued, undeflected, in his church policy. The clergy who supported him, mainly in the region of Aberdeen, moved further in the direction of English practice and ritual. A Jesuit missionary reported the appearance in Scottish churches of organs and altars, the wearing of the surplice and the singing of matins and evensong. The form of worship seemed to him "an imitation of the Mass."[31] The powers of a High Commission Court were now conferred on the Scots bishops, who thus, like the English, acquired the right to discipline the unruly. A new Book of Canons, something on the English model, had been sent to Scotland to replace the *Book of Discipline* of John Knox. These things aroused a muttering resentment, but the opposition had as yet no organisation; the alliance between the nobility, who felt their power and property in danger, and the discontented clergy and laity had not fully come into being.

The Book of Canons, which brought the organisation of the Scots Church into line with that of England, was to be followed by a new Prayer Book which should do the same for the order of worship. It was ready by the year 1636 but on the advice of the King's council in Scotland its introduction was postponed for several months.

The council was divided in opinion. The bishops naturally approved of the Book; several of their fellow councillors did not, and most of them foresaw serious opposition. The Book was presented in a manner bound to offend the sensibilities of the Scots. No Assembly of the Kirk and no Parliament had been called to discuss it, and although it had been drawn up by Scotsmen, they had gone to London to draft it in consultation with the English Archbishop. Furthermore, the King had prefaced it with a royal command to all ministers to use it and a sentence of outlawry on all who refused. A beautiful and dignified liturgy thus reached the Scots in a manner and in a form which could not but be offensive. It looked like an assault on their political as well as their religious independence.

The danger, as the King's council knew, lay as much in the ambitions of the discontented peers as in the religious fervour of people and ministers. What would Rothes and Balmerino do, given the opportunity? Their religious feelings might not go very deep, but suspicion of anything that smacked of Popery touched at once their prejudices, their dearest interests and

seventy years of continuous tradition. As a ruffianly old nobleman said, when religion was discussed: "If I have lain with
never so many whores, I'll never lie with the whore of Babylon."
If the bigotry, greed and ancient feudal authority of the nobles
should come together with the fervour of the people, great
trouble would certainly follow.

For this reason the council asked for postponement, and only
at the repeated instance of the King, at last, and with trepida-
tion, fixed a Sunday at the end of July 1637 for the official
introduction of the new order of worship throughout the
country.

In Scotland and in England dislike and suspicion of Catholicism went with certain simple and far-reaching political prejudices. Both countries had experienced, to a greater or lesser
degree, the reverberations of Europe's religious wars. Both had
recollections of attempted foreign interference in the Roman
Catholic interest, but in England the prejudice against Catholicism was closely linked with the hatred of Spain. It was the
heritage of the Armada and the Elizabethan seamen. When
the King had visited the Isle of Wight as a young man he had
been surprised to see an inn sign representing a friar clawed by
a lion. When he asked its meaning, his host, the genial John
Oglander, boasted "we serve all papists and priests in that
manner."[32] John Oglander was far from being an extreme
Protestant, still less a Puritan; he spoke from the fullness of an
Elizabethan heart.

King Charles made little allowance for such prejudices, and
did not understand the confusion of thought in many of his
subjects' minds. At York he had carefully arranged for the
restoration of the shrine of Saint William; both he and Laud
spoke respectfully of the saints, and it was alleged that a cleric
who had referred disparagingly to Saint George had been made
to apologise for his irreverence. The Archbishop had certainly
prosecuted a man for publishing an almanack in which the
names of Protestant martyrs from Foxe's Book were substituted
for those of saints.

Side by side with the harassing of Calvinists, Baptists and
other Protestant critics of the Church, went a policy of com-

parative toleration for Roman Catholics. In his marriage treaty
the King had undertaken to repeal the more oppressive of the
laws against them. Parliament had compelled him to break this
promise, but in the long intermission of Parliaments after 1630
the King had found a way out. He did not repeal the laws but
he exempted his Catholic subjects by individual letters patent,
in return for a sum of money; this policy was advantageous as
well as tolerant.

In other ways, the laws rusted. It was by law a capital
offence for an English priest to be found in the country, but
priests went openly about London. The Franciscans had returned, theoretically in secret, although their presence was
generally known; the English province had been re-founded,
and the Jesuits, who were jealous, spoke of them as Archbishop
Laud's trencher-flies, a term which seems to have arisen from
Laud's purely intellectual interest in the suggestions put forward by one of them, Franciscus a Sancta Clara, for the recon-
ciliation of the Anglican and the Roman Churches. Another
eminent exile, Mary Ward, the founder of a new religious order
in Germany, the *Englische Fräulein*, came home with a small
band of nuns and found a temporary resting place for them in
Yorkshire.

The Catholic, or potentially Catholic, minority in the
country was still in some districts a large one, able to give help
and protection to the priests. In London, the bulk of the respectable population was strongly Protestant; the priests worked
among the poor, the outcasts and the plague-stricken. Sometimes these London priests were under arrest and lived in prison
awaiting trial, but by day they were allowed out on bail to
perform their priestly functions. The further course of the law
against them was held up indefinitely by the mercy of the King.
This curious situation aroused some critical comparisons with
the plight of one or two Protestant preachers and writers whom
the King's justice had confined to prison without such unofficial
privileges.

In Ireland the penal laws had been temporarily suspended in
return for a large sum of money. Roman Catholics were
allowed to practise at the bar and to hold positions of public

trust. No obstacles were put in the way of the private practice of their religion although public services and large gatherings of the faithful were expressly forbidden, as were also pilgrimages, processions and all open demonstrations of faith.

In Scotland, where the majority was strongly Calvinist, the King's attempts to alleviate the persecution of his Catholic subjects were less successful. The Catholic cause was, for one thing, closely connected with the Gordon clan and its chief the Marquis of Huntly, a circumstance which confused the religious problem with the enmities of the clans and the traditional hostility between highlands and lowlands. All that the King had contrived to do was to grant special privileges to Huntly and his family.

Jesuit missionaries were active in Scotland, and, in the region round Aberdeen where Huntly's power was greatest, they conducted a regular ministry among the faithful. The air of secrecy and conspiracy which surrounded a religion carried on in so limited and dangerous a manner was especially strong in Scotland. In 1630 a principal member of Huntly's family had perished with several companions in a fire at Frendraught, a house belonging to the Crichtons. The Crichtons, though apparently reconciled, were hereditary enemies of the Gordons, and foul play was suspected. If the horrible business had indeed been a murder and not an accident, it was probably the result of personal enmity and nothing more, but a religious motive was half suspected. The Catholics told a tragic tale of the heroism of the young victim who had expounded the true faith to his companions as the flames crept up the tower in which he was trapped. This, with the evident unwillingness of those responsible for justice in Scotland to bring the crime home to the Crichtons, suggested that religious feuds were involved and that Protestant sympathisers were determined to shield the murderers of a prominent Catholic, in spite of all that the King could do to have the culprits punished.[33]

The King's concessions to Catholics might not have provoked so much unfavourable comment from his Protestant subjects had not the open practice of Catholicism at Court attracted general attention. The Queen was the focus of fashionable

Catholicism: a new and elegant allure lit up the old religion, and many lords and ladies flocked to the services in the Queen's chapel at Somerset House. Some went to be in the fashion but some were potential converts. The Queen's confessor, a charming and cultivated Scottish Benedictine, Robert Philip, often debated religious points with interested courtiers, and the exisence of what was almost a Roman Catholic mission at Court made a bad impression on Puritan Londoners. The King, although he was indignant when any of his courtiers became converts, encouraged the intelligent and cultivated priests who surrounded his wife. He dearly loved a theological argument, and these men, unlike the Calvinists, talked a language which he approved and understood. He felt himself in many ways very close to them.

When the Queen had shown him a beautiful diamond cross, a gift sent to her by her godfather Pope Urban VIII, he had smiled and said that he must change his opinion of Roman priests: he had until this time believed that they would take but never give. The innocent jest gave rise to malicious speculation as to what the King had meant by the promise to change his opinion.

With his ideal of unity and uniformity, Charles truly wished to see Catholic Christendom made whole again. But, like the Archbishop and the Laudian clergy, he was convinced that this could only be through concessions made by the Pope to the Anglican communion. He stood out with resolute firmness against the appointment of a Roman Catholic bishop to look after the faithful in England. The establishment of a dual system of bishoprics, Roman and Anglican, would have implied acceptance of schism. Compliments between his Court and the Vatican were, however, frequent, and the Pope presented him with a splendid bust done by the famous Bernini from Van Dyck's painting.

The Vatican had exchanged agents with King Charles's Court in 1636. The King had sent to Rome the Scot Sir William Hamilton an optimistic Roman Catholic who talked hopefully of the coming return of Great Britain to the Church. Father George Con, the Vatican agent in England, was also a Scots-

man but of a more realist temperament: he recognised the
ultimate intransigence of both sides and he was alive to the
strength of Puritan opinion in England. An intelligent and
highly educated man, Con had a threefold attraction for the
King, as a fellow Scotsman, a connoisseur of the arts and a
cultivated conversationalist. Although he had no intention of
changing his religion, Charles received and welcomed him with
friendly familiarity and on one occasion had kept the chapter
of the Knights of the Garter waiting for more than half an
hour while he showed Con some new acquisitions to his collection. The slight to the greatest knightly order in the kingdom
naturally provoked comment.

In other ways the King's affection for his wife and her friends
made him indiscreet. He once accompanied her on a visit to the
small community of Capuchins under her protection at Somerset
House, inspected their chapel and their cells and stayed to share
their humble and friendly supper.[34]

Charles himself, strong in the consciousness of his innocence,
had no patience with the foolish misunderstandings to which
his conduct gave rise, and punished with severity those who
propagated slanders. A man who asserted that the King attended
Mass with the Queen was fined £5,000, but while the King
continued his favours to Roman Catholics, such harshness was
in vain; his critics merely assumed that he chose an occasional
victim to gloss over the awkward truth. Archbishop Laud, who
fully recognised the danger, regretted the King's encouragement
of Con and implored him to restrain the influence of some of
the Queen's other protégés. Two of her courtiers troubled him
especially, Toby Mathew and Wat Montagu; the former was
the son of an Anglican bishop, the latter of the pious and sternly
Protestant Earl of Manchester. Both were recent and eloquent
converts to Rome, and both were clever men. Montagu was
the more serious, Mathew the more amusing. He delighted in
and played up to a reputation for entertaining silliness—as, for
instance, when he offered to make some of the new drink,
chocolate, for the Queen and did indeed do so, but absentmind-
edly drank it all up himself. Under this mask of levity, he was a
man of a keen, inquiring mind, widely read and alert to all the

latest explorations in the sciences. Not the least charm of fashionable Roman Catholicism at this time was that it represented also the *avant-garde* of intellectual life. Lord Herbert of Raglan and Sir Kenelm Digby, both Catholics, stood with Toby Mathew among the foremost amateur scientists of the age, and it was a group consisting principally of Catholics who a few years before, had tried to found a society devoted to the new learning.

The Archbishop was aware of the impression made by the King's encouragement of Roman Catholics. The popular argument was ignorant, incorrect, but deadly: if the King, the head of the Anglican Church, persecuted honest Protestants and smiled upon the Papists, it followed that the Church itself was being led back to Rome. The King's indiscreet and harmless relations with his wife's friends made his, and Laud's, religious policy suspect, not only to extremists and fanatics, but to the substantial majority of his Protestant subjects.

The misapprehension was deepened and embittered by the part which England under King Charles had come to play, or rather *not* to play, in the politics of Europe. Educated men had certain broad conceptions of foreign policy and of England's position and part in European affairs. For the last seventy years western Europe had been divided into two warring camps: the intense struggle between the Habsburg dynasty, ruling in Spain and Austria, and the Bourbon dynasty, ruling in France, had extended and confused the religious wars arising out of the Reformation. The Habsburg dynasty had taken upon themselves a crusade against the heretic; as a result, the French King, although officially Catholic, usually found it wise to sustain the Protestant forces with advice, money and arms, while the Vatican, which also had political interests to consider, tended to support France against Spain. In England this criss-cross of dynastic and religious interests was not widely understood, and the war appeared simply as a religious struggle or as a fight against the dominance of Spain. When, in Elizabeth's time, the English had entered the conflict they had fought against Spanish sea-power which barred their own adventurous expansion in the Americas, and with equal if confused zeal against the Church of Rome and the Spanish Inquisition. The fact that the Roman Catholic powers were not all on the same side in the war, and that the Vatican had moved steadily into alliance with France against Spain, meant very little to the average uninformed Englishman.

The last twenty years had been marked, in Europe, by a resurgence not of the Spanish but of the Austrian Habsburgs who, in the first decade of the Thirty Years War, had regained a large part of central Europe and of the German states for the Catholic Church. The plight of their co-religionists was brought home to the Protestant English by the presence in their midst of refugee German and Bohemian divines, often in such want that they sent their children in quest of alms from door to door. The words "the Protestant Cause" had become a catch-phrase in political discussion. Without very much conception of what the King could do to help the Cause, alehouse politicians—and a fair number of intelligent critics as well—blamed him for doing nothing. In Europe the Protestant Cause was sustained against Spain and Austria in the fields of Germany and Flanders by the Dutch and the Swedes, on the Rhine principally by the French, and at sea, against the Spaniards, by the Dutch alone. The King of England's great ships did nothing more distinguished than squabble with neighbouring Protestant powers about fishing rights.

Clashes with the Dutch in the Narrow Seas and in the Indies, where the merchants of both nations competed for trade, were becoming yearly more violent. But the average Englishman's feeling for the Protestant Cause was stronger than his feelings of rivalry so long as the Dutch were at war with Spain. The Hollanders could still therefore count on English volunteers for their armies and on sympathy from most, if not all, the English people. King Charles's subjects were not so deeply gratified as they should have been when the King, instead of assisting the Protestant Cause, turned his naval guns against the Dutch and with a show of force compelled their government to accept England's prior rights over the herring fisheries. The King, who was anxious to silence critics and to impress on his subjects the importance of what he had done, had a silver medal struck for the occasion. It was a most beautiful piece of work by Briot and bore the lovely text: *Justice and Peace have kissed one another*, but the symbolism represented the intention rather than the achievement of the treaty. The Dutch took little notice of the agreement, and incidents between their fishing boats and the Navy continued much as before.

A Court which favoured the Catholics, a Church which persecuted the Calvinists, a navy which fired only on the Dutch—the simplified picture was open to a dangerous interpretation. Neither at home nor abroad did the policy of King Charles appear Protestant. In the opinion of many it was not even neutral: in 1630 the King had made a treaty with Spain by which Spanish silver was to be minted in England and transported in English ships to Antwerp, where it was needed to pay the Spanish armies which were fighting the Dutch. To Spain the advantage of this arrangement was that the money, shipped by a power which was technically neutral, was safe from interception by the Dutch navy. The advantage to King Charles was that he received a share of each load of bullion for the English mint. This, as the Dutch complained, was a very odd kind of neutrality. In effect the King had become the pensioner and helper of Spain.[85]

The Protestant critics of the King's policy were bound together by the sentimental cult of the King's only sister Elizabeth. She had been married in 1613 to the young Elector Palatine, a Protestant and Calvinist alliance which had been extremely popular. Her husband had some years later accepted the crown of Bohemia from the insurgent Protestants of that country, an action which had precipitated the Habsburg crusade against Protestantism in the imperial dominions. In the course of the struggle the unhappy man had lost not only Bohemia but his title of Elector and all his hereditary German lands. Elizabeth had left behind in her own country a pleasing impression of her youth, liveliness and beauty. This had since been overlaid with visions both noble and tragic: Elizabeth, crowned Protestant Queen of Bohemia; Elizabeth, "our blessed undaunted lady," sharing the rigours of her husband's wintry flight from Prague; Elizabeth, Queen of Hearts, rallying to the drooping Protestant

Cause the chivalry of northern Europe; Elizabeth, a fertile mother of many beautiful children (cheap woodcuts of her with an increasing troop of little ones were very popular in London); finally, Elizabeth the tragic widow defending the forlorn rights of her eldest son. At the core of these visions was a living woman of charm, character and considerable beauty. Those who troubled to make the short journey to The Hague, where she lived as a pensioner of the Dutch government, found their fervour for her cause stimulated by her conversation. A few of the more austere Calvinists were shocked by the frivolity of her family, who were greatly given to acting plays, but most visitors were impressed by her courage and high spirits.

The Queen of Bohemia herself was attached to her brother, King Charles, and was grateful for the help which he sent her. But it was known—how could it be otherwise?—that she regretted his inability or unwillingness to take on her behalf any effective action in war or diplomacy. The visit to the English Court of her son, the Elector Palatine, Charles Louis, had strikingly emphasised the King's failure in this respect. The young man had come seeking help from his uncle, hoping that the King would find the time ripe for intervention in the European war against the Spanish-Austrian power. It was plain for all to see, in the summer of 1637, that he had been turned away, if not quite empty-handed, at least gravely disappointed. He had hoped that a defensive and offensive alliance might be signed with the King of France, now fighting the Spanish-Austrian power on the Rhine, in Flanders and on the Pyrenees, that the English navy would join with the Dutch in the attack on Spanish sea-power, and King Charles take up the part once played by Queen Elizabeth. As nephew of the King he would then have had the help and prestige he needed to regain his father's forfeited lands in Germany.

The King had, however, made difficulties even about recognising the precedence to which, as an Elector, his nephew thought himself entitled, and on one occasion he had to listen to a Court sermon denouncing the Calvinist doctrines in which he had been educated and for which his father had fought. The

King, after a brief wavering in the direction of an alliance with France against Spain and Austria, had sunk again into his uncertain neutrality. "Mutability and confusion reign here," lamented the Venetian envoy, while the Spaniard, in a burst of rage at the King's vacillations, declared to a fellow ambassador that no Court in the world conducted diplomacy so strangely as did the English; they did not listen, they did not understand, and they changed their opinions at every moment. A wild scheme by which the Elector's younger brother Rupert was to command a fleet for the conquest of Madagascar was all the talk of the Court for some weeks, and Davenant celebrated the imaginary venture in a poem. At another time the King spoke of placing fifteen warships at the disposal of the Elector. But in the end Charles continued to devote his naval energies to the herring quarrel with the Dutch, while all that he gave the young Elector was advice to go to the wars himself and make a reputation. He was, at least, generous about personal allowances to both the princes, and added a sizeable lump sum with which the Elector could hire some soldiers, but, as his courtiers said, he was willing to pay to get rid of his poor relations.[36]

The Elector had a cool head and a cool heart. Early in the proceedings King Charles had had to reprimand the young man's secretaries for putting too many military and diplomatic schemes into his head. The reprimand may have been intended for the Elector himself, who was thereafter no less active but more discreet. He privately canvassed the opinions of the Venetian and Dutch ambassadors in London on his own affairs and his uncle's policy.[37] He also cultivated the friendship of the more eminent Protestant critics of the King, especially those with naval and colonial interests.

The alliance of colonial adventure with militant Protestantism, which had sprung from the first clashes of English seamen with Spain, had grown stronger when the policy of the Crown became favourable to Catholics at home and to Spain abroad. English naval enterprise of late, had developed in a manner likely to prove dangerous should it come to an open conflict between the Court and its critics. By the peace with Spain in 1604 King James I had relinquished the claim of Englishmen to trade in the West Indies. Undeterred, English captains continued to trade under foreign flags. They used as their bases ports in the Netherlands, in southern Ireland and in North Devon. The illicit nature of their traffic made them bold, self-reliant and unscrupulous. Fiercely conscious of their English race, reputation and religion, they were at the same time indifferent to and contemptuous of the authority of the royal government, which neither recognised nor protected them. One of England's major commercial interests and one of the chief sources of national and local pride thus eluded the royal authority altogether. A new tradition, which had ripened through a long generation, had created something like an opposition, rather than a loyalty, between the most adventurous English seamen and the Crown. While the King struck pretentious medals about herring treaties, his subjects defied Spain, the traditional enemy, at their own expense and under any flag but their own.

Foremost of the men who financed and sometimes took part in this underhand expansion of sea-power was Robert Rich, Earl of Warwick. He was the son of Penelope Devereux, immortal as the *Stella* of Sir Philip Sidney's poems. By her unloved husband ("that Rich fool, who by blind fortune's lot, the richest gem of love and life enjoys") Penelope had been the mother of two sons—this Robert, and a younger, Henry, now Earl of Holland and a favourite of Queen Henrietta Maria. By her lover, the Earl of Devonshire, Penelope had had a third son. Mountjoy Blount, now Earl of Newport and a prominent man at Court. These three men were on friendly family terms with their cousin, the living Earl of Essex, Penelope's brother's son. Another friend, the Earl of Hertford, had married the Earl of Essex's sister. Of this family group Holland and Newport alone were figures at Court. Warwick, an active seaman who had himself once led an expedition to the West Indies, preferred his country houses and the ships and dockyards to Hampton Court and Whitehall. Essex and Hertford had both as young men suffered humiliation and unhappiness at the hands of the Court. Essex, at twenty-four, had been compelled by King James I to allow his wife, whom the King's favourite wished to marry, to divorce him on the score of impotence. He had served in the Low Countries since then and had the reputation of a good soldier, a good Protestant and an honest unpretentious fellow. Hertford had in youth loved and secretly married the Lady Arabella Stuart, cousin of King James. The alliance had been thought to endanger the throne to which Arabella and Hertford had each a tenuous claim. The lovers were parted, Hertford fled the country and Arabella died, mad, in the Tower. At fifty his tragic romance was a thing of memory; he was comfortably re-married to the sister of Essex, and the father of a family—a stodgy, uninspired gentleman of Protestant views, neither in nor out of favour with the Court, but not particularly attached to it.

These kinsmen had other associates and friends, Lord Saye and Seal, Lord Brooke, John Hampden a rich Buckinghamshire landowner, and John Pym a West country squire of great business ability. Both these latter had been prominent opponents of the King in the last Parliament and all were active in advocating and financing colonial ventures.

The Elizabethan wars with Spain had created the alliance between strong Protestantism and colonial expansion of which these men were the most outstanding representatives. At home, they protected and encouraged the Protestant clergy. In the settlements across the Atlantic they placed ministers of the same kind. New England was becoming a refuge centre for laymen and clergy unwilling to accept the Laudian rule; astonishing in its religious and intellectual vigour, the little settlement of Boston had already in 1636 founded a college for Puritan theology and Puritan learning in the New World. John Harvard, graduate of Emmanuel College, Cambridge, the chief centre of Puritan thought at home, had left four hundred books and seven hundred pounds to create a second Cambridge by the Charles river in Massachusetts.

But the ideals and interests of the leading Puritan-adventurers and their antagonism to the Crown were concentrated in particular in the Caribbean settlements controlled by the Providence Company of which Warwick, Saye, Brooke and Hampden were all shareholders. Warwick's courtier brother Lord Holland, another shareholder, protected the company's interests at Whitehall. Oliver St. John, a leading Puritan barrister, was the company's solicitor and its secretary was John Pym.

The Company had founded the settlement of Providence, on the small Caribbean island now known as Santa Catalina, with a two-fold intention. The outpost, with its two neighbouring islands Association and Henrietta, was well placed as a naval base for the harrying of Spain; but the new settlements were also to be models of primitive virtue. In Providence, Henrietta and Association sin would be unknown and simple purity reign supreme. The Company drew up regulations, forbidding cards and dice and permitting only chess as an evening recreation for the people, with other stern and simple rules. Whoring, drunkenness, profanity would not be tolerated. A carefully chosen minister—a German Calvinist refugee from the Palatinate—was brought home in disgrace for singing catches on a Sunday.

The business of these three godly settlements was chiefly to keep watch on Spanish ships and prey on them when possible. The Earl of Warwick and his friends were sincerely trying to create three nests of pirates with the behaviour and morals of a Calvinist theological seminary. Other difficulties beside the moral ones afflicted the Providence settlements. Only negroes could work effectively in the climate, but this involved the company in the African slave trade; moreover the negroes grew mutinous and further importation had to be stopped. There was little water. A plague of rats swept the settlements. The cultivation of tobacco and cotton both failed to pay—tobacco because of the King's interference with the trade, and cotton because the means to dress the raw material for export were lacking. Fruit and sugar canes alone seemed to do well, and hogs throve. But Spanish, French and Dutch hostility menaced the islands on every side, and in 1635 the Spaniards raided and totally destroyed the settlement at Association.

The shareholders of the Company met in London, either at Lord Brooke's house or at Warwick's; John Pym was at one or other of the houses more often than the rest, for the main burden of organisation rested on him. He was an efficient manager and administrator, with a quick, resourceful wit, a good memory, and an astonishing capacity for acquiring, digesting and using information.

The shareholders of the Providence Company undoubtedly talked politics together. They could hardly have avoided it, since their religious and colonial interests were so much affected by the King's church policy and by his friendship with Spain. Some or all of them certainly paid their respects to the Elector Palatine during his long and disappointing visit to his uncle's Court. At one moment during that visit, the King, in a tentative movement towards a change of foreign policy, went so far as to give verbal consent to a war of reprisals on the Spaniards in the Caribbean—a war to be waged at the Company's expense and with its own ships. Faced with a continual tale of loss and disaster, the Company had considered moving the colony to the mainland but the possibility of recouping their losses through licensed piracy brightened the outlook, and in the summer of 1637 the shareholders sank another £100,000 in the enterprise and decided to go on with it.[38] Their original ideals had dismally faded and an enterprise which had begun with the genuine intention of planting a godly commonwealth, had deteriorated into a scheme for licensing pirate captains in return for a share of the profits. The records of the Providence Company are depressing, but it was, for all that, the heir of the Elizabethan tradition.

The King's private permission to the governors of the company to pursue their own war on Spain did not in their eyes counterbalance the rest of his foreign policy. Saye, Brooke, Warwick, Hampden, Pym and their friends felt as strongly as any in England that in failing to support the Elector Palatine the King was betraying the Protestant Cause and losing the opportunity of a war both profitable, honourable and just.

The King's religious policy and his foreign policy worked together to increase the misgivings of his opponents about the future of their country under his unquestioned rule. A small fact, a mere accident, to which Prynne had drawn attention in his *News from Ipswich*, seemed to clinch the matter. In the reissue of the Prayer Book for the year 1636 the prayer for

Elizabeth, Queen of Bohemia, and her family had been omitted. Prayers for the King's sister had been said as long as Charles was childless and she was heiress-presumptive to the throne. By 1636 he had five living children; the number of his relations who could reasonably be included by name in a prayer was naturally limited, but the exclusion of Elizabeth was loaded with dark significance by her brother's critics.

The King treated such follies with contempt, but he was mistaken in doing so. The various parts of his policy were open not simply to misinterpretation, but to the *same* misinterpretation. There lay the danger: his religious policy and his foreign policy united too many of his subjects in the same resentments and the same fears.

III. THE KING'S PEACE AND THE

KING'S REVENUE

The distrust created by the King's church policy would have been less damaging to his prospects had he been successful in practical administration. A government which is not trusted can be effective only if it is feared, and Charles might have achieved something of what he wished to achieve had his administration been conducted in such a manner as to command respect and compel obedience.

England was the richest, most influential and most valuable of his dominions, and on English administration his true power was based. No reputable English lawyer would at this time have contested the proposition that "the law of Royal Government is a law fundamental."[1] But the way in which this government was to be exercised gave rise to argument. The King believed that it rested with his good will alone to respect and uphold his people's liberties, but a contemporary legal work aptly expressed another view, "English laws are rather popular than peremptory, rather accepted than exacted."[2] In practice the administration of the laws rested on the consent and co-operation of the King's subjects, countrymen and citizens, justices of the peace, constables, sheriffs and lords lieutenant throughout the country, to whom power was delegated. "The authority of a King is the keystone which closeth up the arch of government," one of the King's principal supporters had said. But the arch was made up of many other stones beside the keystone. To change the metaphor: the King was the fountain of justice. But the river of justice which flowed from the monarch divided into multitudinous smaller streams and canals irrigating the whole country, with, as it were, their own locks, weirs and fishing rights: they retained only a theoretical and remote consciousness of the fountain whence their waters came.

The King personally appointed the judges, whose first duty, as he saw it, was to maintain his authority. Francis Bacon, his father's Chancellor, had described the judges as "lions under the throne." If the lions roared in such a manner as to shake rather than support the throne, it was plain sense, and plain duty, to silence them. Neither James I nor Charles I had hesitated to do so. James had removed Lord Chief Justice Coke, the loud-mouthed champion of the common law, and Charles dismissed Lord Chief Justice Crewe when he refused to uphold the legality of one of the royal demands for money. To make his authority over the judicial bench clear beyond doubt the King had altered the formula by which judges were appointed. In the past judges had held office *quamdiu se bene gesserint*, or as long as they behaved rightly. In King Charles's time the judges were appointed *durante bene placito*, or during the King's good pleasure.

The King was careful to discourage all studies which seemed likely to produce a wrong attitude in lawyers. The antiquary Sir Robert Cotton found warrant in Anglo-Saxon institutions and in the baronial wars of Henry III for doctrines of government unfavourable to the King; his library was impounded and he himself excluded from Court favour. The King also prohibited further publication of Sir Edward Coke's commentaries on the laws, seized his papers and relegated the ex-Chief Justice to apoplectic silence in a country exile.

Such actions would have been politic had the King found nominees of worth and character to fill the Bench, but his choice fell too often upon the merely ambitious, the complaisant, or those with money to offer. John Finch and John Bramston, who had been the Chief Justices since 1635, were learned and ingenious lawyers, but Finch was too unscrupulous, vain and ambitious to command respect, and Bramston was weak and malleable. Edward Littleton and John Bankes, respectively Solicitor-General and Attorney-General, were men of greater integrity; these were respectable appointments. But as a rule the prices of remunerative places were whispered round Whitehall and the prospects of the bidders openly discussed for months at a time.[3]

While, as lions under the throne, the judges grew to look like sheep or even jackals, respect for them declined. This did not affect the popular esteem in which the law was held, for the law had an existence independent of the King's theories or the corruption of the Bench, and therein lay its strength.

Justice was administered throughout the kingdom in a multitude of small local courts, and the governors of England, in all that affected the daily life of the subject, were the local justices of the peace—small gentry in the countryside, aldermen in the cities. At Quarter Sessions the justices, gathered together in the county town, fixed the rate of wages and discussed the state and needs of the county. They were competent to ·ry all crimes except treason or offences by the King's servants. These cases, together with a few which presented exceptional problems of law, would be reserved for trial by the King's judges at the Assizes.

Between sessions the justices saw to the daily affairs of the village, apprenticed boys to trades, disciplined unruly servants, ordered idlers into the fields at harvest time, licensed or suppressed alehouses, punished rogues and vagabonds, put bastard children out to nurse, sent lewd women and incorrigible beggars to the house of correction, relieved the sick, poor and disabled, encouraged lawful and discouraged unlawful sports, and saw to the maintenance—such as it was—of roads and bridges.

The innumerable petty disputes over boundaries and trespass, which occurred in a countryside very little enclosed and cultivated on the strip system, were mostly settled by the old manorial courts—the Court Leet or the Court Baron—both of which still survived. Here the lord of the manor or his steward sat in the chair of justice, to deal with trespass, poaching, and injury to park land, but also to rebuke eavesdroppers, scolds, drunkards and trouble-makers.

Neither lords of manors, stewards nor justices of the peace in town or country were by custom or necessity deeply versed in the law, though many of them had been for a while at the Inns of Court in London. The little learning they had then acquired,